Greek text edited by Athena Dountsi
English translation by Cox and Solman, Athens

Photographs by Dimitris Talianis
and Vassilis Tsonis

ISBN: 960-7646-04-5
© Dimitris Talianis, Topio Publications, 1996
11 Kountouriotou St, 17122 N. Smyrni, Greece, tel. (01) 9307641, fax 9307642

ARTEMIS SKOUBOURDIS

Tour guide - historian

ATHENS

HISTORY · ART · MONUMENTS

TOPIO PUBLICATIONS

Our thanks for their kind permission to use material to:

The National Archaeological Museum
The National Historical Museum
The National Gallery
The Academy of Athens
The Acropolis Museum
The Kerameikos Museum
The Benaki Museum
The City of Athens Museum
The Athenian Club
Ekdotike Athenon
Kiki Vassiliou
Apostolos Doxiadis
Eleni Leptourgos

Cover illustration: The Arrival of King Othon - The Temple of Hephaestus, Peter von Hess, 1835, oils. In the State Art Gallery, Munich (reproduced from History of the Greek Nation, Ekdotike Athenon, vol. XIII).

Front end-paper illustration: View of Athens with the Aqueduct of Hadrian, Louis François Cassas, coloured engraving, City of Athens Museum.

Illustration on page 6: Panoramic View of Athens, Joseph Schranz, 1840, water-colour. City of Athens Museum.

To my parents:
advocates of life, and of life lived well

*A*thens, Hymettus, Lycabettus, Ilissus, Cephisus, salpinx, zephyr, triumph, rose, hyacinth, narcissus: words that come into English from Greek, and predate the Greeks themselves; they have been used for 6,000 years now, a period as long as the history of Athens itself. For thousands of years they have echoed in the magical city of Athens, and they echo the fruitful presence of the Pelasgians, first inhabitants of the site. Two thousand years before Christ, the Pelasgians gave way to the Greeks, the Ionian Athenians who took the city to the triumphs of the Golden Age. And since then, roses, hyacinths and narcissi have blown in the zephyrs, scenting the air of Athens.

Athens lies in a basin surrounded by lines of mountains, most of which are limestone and crystalline. To the north is mount Parnes, to the west stand the hills of Aegaleo, to the north-east rises Mount Pentelikon —renowned since antiquity for its white marble— and to the east looms Hymettus, which can shift colour so rapidly, especially towards sunset, that it has been called *the mad mountain*. Athens is the city of eleven hills: the Tourkovounia to the north, Lycabettus, Strefi hill, Colonus in the Agora, the Areopagus, the hills of the Nymphs and Philopappus, the Pnyx, Ardettos and the 'Sicilian hillocks' to the south, and dominating in the centre, the rock of the Acropolis, Pindar's "marvellous city".

'Thin-soiled' Athens is cooled by famous rivers, largely seasonal in nature: the Ilissus and the Cephisus, whom the Athenians revered as gods and whose figures were carved for posterity by Phidias on the Parthenon. The third river, the Eridanus, has run dry now; the last traces of its waters can be detected in the ancient cemetery of Kerameikos. There were springs around the Sacred Rock, Clepsydra, the Mycenean Spring, the Archaic Spring of the Asclepeion, and these, with the nine-mouthed Callirhoe spring, quenched the thirst of the Athenians in the drought years.

The environment, nature, the outstanding climate, the clarity of the atmosphere, the sunny days that followed moonlit nights, and the cool breeze from the Aegean, were all among the elements that shaped the Athens of antiquity, the city whose spirit and soul would conquer mankind.

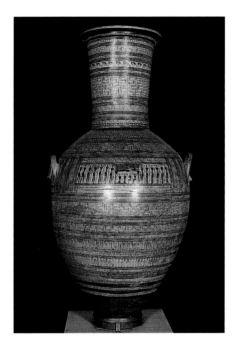

THE DIPYLON AMPHORA.

An outstanding example of the Geometric art of Athens, from around 800 BC. The Mycenean plant motifs have begun to change and become more stylised, before ultimately evolving into geometrical shapes. A new aesthetic concept is quite clear in this artistic expression -as is the continuity between the Mycenean past the Geometric present. (Archaeolog. Museum)

THE DIPYLON KOUROS.

A work characteristic of the difficult years of Draconian legislation. The hair is tightly curled and organised along horizontal and perpendicular axes and the large, almond-shaped eyes are those of a boy just awakened from a sleep of confused dreams; they are in a hurry to get to know the world and conquer it. (Archaeological Museum)

THE CITY IS BORN - THE HARD YEARS

In prehistoric Athens, history blends into mythology to generate very fascinating legends. Poseidon vied with Athena for the city, it is said, one offering water and the other the olive to its inhabitants. They chose Athena's olive, and were called 'Athenians'.

Cecrops was the founder and first king of the city. He was followed by Pandion, Erechtheus and Aegeus —men and chthonic deities together, who reconciled and amalgamated the old pre-Greek cults with the newcomers from Olympus. Theseus, son of Aegeus, brought glory to the city and in killing the Minotaur released Athens from its obligation to pay tribute to King Minos. The most important achievement of Theseus was the *synoecia*, the unification of the demes of Attica under the sceptre of the King of Athens. Thus he created Athens, a city with a plural name, and strengthened the institution of the city-state.

Yet, although it flourished in Mycenean times, Athens wasn't particularly important as a power in Greece as a whole. This was reasonable enough: other cities paled beside the might of Homer's "Mycenae, rich in gold". Nonetheless, the art of Athens (and of Attica in general) stood out for its elegance and high quality, and also displayed features which it was to retain throughout its history: regularity, and clarity that omitted everything superfluous.

According to the traditions, Codrus was the last king of Athens, and his reign is associated with the invasion of the Dorians, in around 1100 BC. When the Dorians (Greeks of a different tribe) were close enough to be a threat to Athens, the Delphic oracle pronounced that "the winning army will be that whose king is killed", whereupon Codrus disguised himself as a villager and went out to taunt the invaders who, unsuspecting, killed him. News had come to them of the oracle, too, and when they discovered Codrus' identity they hastened to fall back from Athena's city without giving battle. And so, Athens remained Ionian, and the fact that no Dorian had set foot in their city was a source of pride to the Athenians.

Although Codrus is traditionally called the last king of Athens, history also tells of Acastus, a later figure credited with leading the campaign to abolish the hereditary monarchy. In fact, it was changing socio-political conditions that caused the shift from monarchy to oligarchy. Under the new regime, when the aristocrats came to power, the role of the Acropolis changed, too. The Acropolis (literally, the *highest point of the city*) ceased to be the location of the king's palace: now it became the city's religious centre, a role it was to retain down even to Christian times.

As these things were happening up on the Acropolis, down in the city the situation was worsening. The aristocrats exerted oppressive rule over the suffering citizens. In order to survive, ordinary people were driven into debt —often reaching the tragic point of mortgaging their own bodies, becoming slaves when they defaulted on their obligations.

While this state of political turmoil lasted, the art of Athens was in what is called the Geometric period, producing vases which stand out for their unique quality. Horizontal and perpendicular lines are set off against accentuating and secondary features in a balance which was always to be characteristic of Greek art.

THE GREAT YEARS BEGIN

This period was followed by the Archaic era, with its great achievements. In Athens, however, the troubles continued, with the oligarchy and the strict laws of Draco (hence 'draconian') tormenting the citizens. It was their good fortune that early in the sixth century BC, Solon, the poet, legislator and pioneer of democracy, made his appearance on the political scene. When he came to power, he introduced a series of laws to benefit the poor, and by the measure that went down in history as the *seisachtheia* (literally, 'lifting of the burdens') cancelled the debts that were crushing the Athenians. Land was redistributed, and a ban placed on the mortgaging of property and the human body. Solon also founded the *ecclesia* of

THE MOSCHOPHORUS.
This statue of a man carrying a calf (570 BC) is as vivid today as it was in ancient times, and a glance is enough to captivate the viewer. Carved out of Athenian marble, this Archaic work is tenderly affectionate. The eyes, full of light and with a profoundly human smile, seem to give life to the handsome, clever face —which is lent still more intelligence by the contrast between it and the passive expression of the calf. Athens, the light, is here. (Acropolis Museum)

the deme —the assembly of the Athenians, that is— and the Heliaea, the people's court. Each Athenian was given the right to elect and be elected, but, since positions of power were not salaried, this meant in practice that only the wealthiest of the citizens could respond to the democratic challenge.

Solon's legislation was revolutionary for its time, and it made him enemies. The aristocrats saw their power waning with each passing day, while the strength of the rich class of merchants and craftsmen increased. The road to tyranny was open: all that was needed was the right person. In the person of the experienced politician Pisistratus, the opponents of Solon found the man they wanted. He managed to trick his way into power, and he and his sons Hipparchus and Hippias ruled the city as dictators for almost half a century (560 - 511 BC).

However, the years of tyranny did have some beneficial effects. Trade and industry flourished, colonies were founded, and the mining of silver at Laurion began. The tyrants looked kindly on the arts and letters. They opened the world's first public library, and Athens was ornamented with new temples, public buildings, fountains and gardens. Architecture and the plastic arts gained a sense of the monumental, and set a firm course for the perfection that was to follow in the Classical era. Nature, history, human life: everything was governed by the laws of perpetual flux, of never-ending change.

The Athenians of the Archaic period had begun to become aware of the fateful change that leads to decay and death, and they reacted by putting forward forms that were incorruptible, static and symmetrical, as expressed in the kouros and the kore —stylised statues of youths and maidens. Pottery, too, took great strides forward, generating the black-figure style in 630 BC and then moving on to the achievements of the red-figure style in 525 BC. By the middle of the sixth century BC, Athens was acknowledged as the principal centre for ceramics in the Mediterranean. The compositions painted on the vases possessed such rhythm, strength

KORE.
The figure in the statue is becoming aware of itself. The expression is deeply spiritual -no coincidence, since the work dates from the time when Tragedy was being born. (Acropolis Museum)

and impetuosity that they sometimes spilled out of the 'frame' left for them on the surface of the pottery.

The Athens of the Archaic period led the way in the theatre, too, with the first drama contests being established in 534 BC. In Athens, something really different was happening: a process of cultural evolution lasting centuries was coming to fruition, producing an unrivalled culture that was to change the face of the world.

This whirlwind of progress swept away the tyrannical regime. In 513 BC, Harmodius and Aristogeiton assassinated Hipparchus and established themselves as national heroes. Hippias clung on to power for three more years, but eventually had to flee to Persia. The end of tyranny had come. In 508-7 BC, Cleisthenes laid the foundations of Athenian democracy, guaranteeing all citizens freedom, equality before the law, and equality of civil rights. The Athenians were divided into ten 'tribes' and governed their own city, each 'tribe' being in charge of affairs for one-tenth of the year. Public offices were assigned by lot and salaried, and each Athenian citizen had the right to elect and be elected.

The battles of Marathon, Salamis and Plataeae were the epic achievements of the Athenians. There, as the vanguard of the Greeks, they humiliated the military might of Persia and drove the invaders from the east off Greek soil.

Art now passed into a period known as the 'severe style': the faces of the statues become grim and lose their 'Archaic smile' in a quite understandable psychological reaction to the menace to the Greeks.

THE GOLDEN AGE

In the Golden Age, the political giants called Miltiades, Aristides, Themistocles and Pericles lived and worked in parallel with the great poets Aeschylus, Sophocles, Euripides and Aristophanes, were the friends of philosophers of the importance of Protagoras, Anaxagoras and Socrates, and might be found at dinner with artists such as Critius, Myron, Phidias, Agoracritus or Alcmenes or major archi-

THE CRITIAN BOY (485-480 BC)
Here we have a wise and self-aware young citizen of Athens, one who rules his own city by taking a positive part in the Ecclesia of the Deme, the Agora and the Bouleuterion. Now the human body has broken free of the stiffness of Archaic art and has gain-ed movement -just as the citizens of Athens threw themselves into poli-tical and social action when democra-cy was taking its first steps.
In the harmoniously balanced torso, whose diagonal axes intersect in a re-flection of the body's movement (the technique known as contraposto), we see expressed the "reciprocal harmo-ny" of Heraclitus: "the cosmic order can be maintained only if a change in one direction involves a correspon-ding change in another direction".
There can be no doubt that this Athenian youth is the world's first free citizen. He is a free citizen of the world, and he expresses the timeless values that were born and matured in the Athens of the fifth century BC, which still shine out in our days of decline, and which mankind will honour in perpetuity.
(Acropolis Museum)

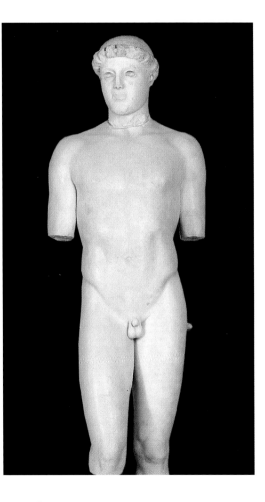

tects like Iktinus, Callicrates and Mnesicles. They, and thousands more of the famous or the anonymous Athenians of the Golden Age, were the creators of the Athenian miracle. And when Pericles came to power, Athens reached the zenith of its fame and glory.

In the city, Democracy, Philosophy, Poetry and all the forms of art were equally honoured. The Parthenon is the embodiment in stone of the striving towards existence and the light of the Athenians of the fifth century BC. On the Parthenon frieze, it is as if the idealised figures of gods and mortal men were leading Athens into the Classical period of art.

But the outbreak of the Peloponnesian War dealt a blow to Athenian leadership, to democracy, and to the arts and letters from which the city never recovered. The undying political rivalry of Athens and Sparta was the cause of civil strife which racked all Greece and lasted 27 whole years. Athens was the chief loser, but democracy and the Greek civilisation also suffered in a conflict that Sparta itself gained little from. The funeral address that Pericles delivered over the dead of the second year of the War —and which Thucydides wrote down shortly before hostilities ended, in 404 BC— was also a requiem and epitaph for the Athenian state. The golden years had gone, never to return. Athens was now heading down the road to turmoil and decay, with only occasional flashes of her former brilliance.

RECONSTRUCTION - THE SECOND CLASSICAL PERIOD

As the century dawned, the prosperity of the previous period must have seemed like a dream to the city and its people. Athens was an impoverished and insignificant ally of Sparta, her walls had been broken down, her fields lay fallow, and her harbours were empty where once they had bustled with the war armada and the commercial fleet. In the years that followed, Athens and the democratic system struggled to put themselves together. The Athenian League was refounded in 378 BC, and Athens became the cradle of philosophy, serving as a magnet for all the

THE PARTHENON FRIEZE, detail (Acropolis Museum).
These superb figures, sculpted by the skilled hand of Phidias, have been marching for centuries along the frieze of the Parthenon, eternal witnesses to a unique age which created and gave prominence to Democracy, Tragedy and the concept of moderation in human affairs.

17

great thinkers -from Aristotle to Zeno and the innovator Epicurus- who came to the city to teach. Plato had already founded his Academy, where rich young men from all over the known world would receive their education down to the very end of antiquity. The plastic arts also flourished, and Athens was able to boast some notable sculptors who continued the brilliant traditions of the golden years. They included Cephisodotus and, later, his famous son Praxiteles, who bestowed greater delicacy of expression and tenderness upon the art of Attica. Praxiteles, Timotheus, Scopas and Leochares (the last three were more realistic in their depictions) were worthy successors to the great Phidias himself. Rhetoric, too, was an area in which strides forward were made in fourth century Athens. Andocides, Lysias, Isaeus, Isocrates, Hyperides, Lycurgus, Aeschines and Demosthenes were among the most famous Athenian orators. In the time of the orator Lycurgus, democracy flowered for a second, and last, time. The city became once more the intellectual centre of the ancient world, one huge school of literature, philosophy and the arts. This role in artistic and intellectual affairs was to persist until the end of antiquity.

The battle of Chaeronea (338 BC), at which the forces of southern Greece were defeated by those of the north, marked the end of Athenian power and the beginning of Macedonian rule. Yet Alexander the Great displayed respect for Athens, and took its culture with him on his campaigns through Asia. The premature death of the Macedonian king, in 323 BC, coincided with the end of democracy in Athens. The periods which followed —the Hellenistic era and Roman times— were years of turmoil, of shoddiness and moral and ethical decline. Of the Athens of Pericles, only the renown and the intellectual standing remained.

ATHENS REBORN

Perhaps the only positive element in the period of Roman rule (146 BC-330 AD) was that the Greeks acquired an awareness of themselves as a nation. There was progress, too, in the realm of women's rights: Plutarch tells us that Greek women

DEXILEOS (394-3 BC) A work typical of what was for the Athenians a tragic age. The boldness of his pose and the profundity of thought manifest in his face reflects the concern widespread among his fellow-citizens. (Kerameikos Museum)

began to receive education at that time, and became rather more independent. Roman Athens was still a centre of learning, and it conquered the souls and minds of the Romans. As the poet Horace puts it, "captive Greece conquered the conqueror who had captured her".

Athenian history experienced one of its darkest moments in the time of the Roman general Sulla. In March of 86 BC, after a siege lasting months, Sulla captured and looted the city. After bearing the brunt of his wrath, there was nothing that could be done to restore Athens, despite the munificence of Julius Caesar and Caesar Augustus. Horace was right to call Athens "an empty city"; Ovid, too, mourned its decay. In 54 AD, St Paul preached on the Areopagus hill, revealing to the Athenians the nature of the unknown god to whom they had erected an altar. But he stirred little interest in the "city wholly given to idolatry", and the only people to espouse the new religion were the Areopagite Dionysius and a woman called Thamar or Damaris.

The second century of the Christian era was a good time for the city of Pallas Athena. Roman and Athenian political, intellectual and financial personalities contributed to the revival of the 'renowned city'. Foremost in this sphere was the Emperor Hadrian (117-138 AD), who adorned Athens with superb monuments such as the Temple of Olympian Zeus, the Pantheon, the Panhellenion, the Library which bears his name and, perhaps most importantly of all, the Aqueduct. The Athenians rightly worshipped him as a god, called him 'Soter' (saviour), and erected in his honour the triumphal Arch of Hadrian. The Arch marks the boundary between the 'city of Theseus' and the new 'city of Hadrian' which was constructed on the recommendation of the Emperor.

This atmosphere was further enhanced by two eminent Athenian patrons of the arts, Julius Atticus and his son Herodes Atticus. The younger man went so far as to renovate the Panathenaic Stadium, adding to it a facing of Pentelic marble, and built the magnificent Odeion which bears his name in memory of his wife.

The successors of Hadrian, Antoninus Pius and Marcus Aurelius, erected public buildings of their own in Athens, and supported the arts and letters in an attempt to approximate to the Athenian splendour of the golden age. Athens became once again the world's university. This was the Athens of Plutarch, and of Pausanias with his arid descriptions of the unrivalled glories of Pericles' time. The Athenians resembled the audience at some theatrical performance consisting of heroic memories to which they themselves were unable to add anything: "they follow, not judging or debating, not even holding elections, but merely following".

This time of comparative prosperity was followed by a further dip in the fortunes of Athens —a dip which became a plunge when the barbarians appeared. In the middle of the third century AD, hordes of Goths flooded across Greece, and in 267 AD the Heruli left a trail of death and destruction.

In the face of imminent disaster, the Athenian philosopher and orator Poplius Herenius Dexippus formed 2,000 of his fellow-citizens into an armed force and succeeded in driving back the barbarians. But the damage had been done. Athens, the city of marble with its fine public buildings, was no more than a memory. The Athenians built a short and makeshift wall behind which they took shelter —and attempted to get on with their lives.

THE QUEEN OF CITIES OVERSHADOWS ATHENS

In 330 AD, the Byzantine Empire was born. The Emperor Constantine the Great, on the throne of the Eastern Roman Empire, chose to built his new capital on the site of the ancient Megarian colony of Byzantium, thus securing the survival of the Greek race.

Athens kept alive its university, "the jewel in the crown of the Greek world and the last bastion of ancient Hellenism". Even the Emperors and the Church Fathers who were most outspoken in their opposition to the pagans, who dealt blow after fatal blow to the ancient sanctuaries, showed some respect for Athens. The religious toleration of the Athenians allowed Christians and pagans to live side-by-side in relative peace.

In the second half of the fifth century, the city had the good fortune to see one of its daughters, Athenais-Eudocia, on the throne of Byzantium as the consort of Theodosius II. Athenais embraced the new religion and was a benefactor to her city, while at the same time helping to consolidate the Greek systems of education and justice and the Greek language in the schools of Constantinople. Her removal from the Byzantine throne was the beginning of the end for Athens. Theodosius stripped the city of its works of art, shipping the finest items to Constantinople. As the star of the Queen of Cities shone more and more brightly, the sun of Athens began to fade, and the city lost its prestige.

ATHENS DISHONOURED AND FORGOTTEN

In 529 AD, the Emperor Justinian delivered the coup de grace, with a decree in which he ordered the closure of the schools of philosophy and the pagan sanctuaries. The cross of Christianity had triumphed over the statues of the gods, and all the ancient temples of the 'great city' were turned into Christian churches —a process in which the belatedly zealous Christian Athenians did much damage to the buildings. Athens then became a 'tiny, insignificant town', a state in which it slumbered for centuries until 1018, when it was awakened by the Emperor Basil the Bulgar-Slayer, who visited the city to celebrate his victories over the Bulgars. A brief period of prosperity began, and lasted until the middle of the twelfth century. Some fine churches were built, and a few have even survived into modern times as outstanding examples of Byzantine art. But by the late twelfth century Athens was a miserable village again. Even in those conditions, Acominatus could still find precious treasures: "The landscape continues to be charming, Hymettus is rich in honey, Piraeus is serene, Eleusis is mysterious, and there is the Acropolis".

THE TOWER OF THE WINDS, Roman Agora. Engraving, Stuart and Revett, 1762.

Those features were sufficient to cause him to adore the city, and bewail its capture by the 'Franks' in 1204. From that year until the Turkish conquest in 1456, Athens was ruled by the 'Franks' —men of varying degrees of culture from right across Western Europe, some of them regular soldiers and some of them mercenaries. With the supposed ultimate aim of freeing the Holy Land from the Arabs, they occupied Greece and shared the land out amongst themselves. 'Franks' of three different nationalities ruled Athens. The first dynasty consisted of the French dukes de la Roche and de la Brienne (1204-1311). Under their sovereignty, there was some degree of security in the city, since the pirates of the Aegean had been suppressed. Athens became a fairy-tale medieval city for a century. But the French were followed by the uncouth Catalan Company (1311-1387), under whom the Athenians were subjected to "an extreme of slavery". As a result, the Florentine Acciaioli dukes who reigned from 1387 to 1456 were a source of moral and financial relief for the Athenians.

In the meantime, the crescent moon of the Turks had risen high in the sky, touching the sun and bursting into a flame that seared Constantinople, which the West had forgotten. In 1453, the cry, "The Queen of Cities is fallen" resounded throughout the Balkans, and the fall of Athens followed three years later. The Sultan was able to exploit the squabbling among the Florentines to place Athens under Turkish control. As Rûm (Byzantium) and Athens declined into the darkness of Turkish rule, the light moved on elsewhere: to the Italy of the Renaissance, where it shone brightly on the birth of the heralds of the future, of Leonardo, of Michelangelo and of Raphael.

In September 1458, Sultan Mohammed the Conqueror visited the city "of ruins and remains". Mohammed was a learned and diplomatic man who admired the city and wished to appease its inhabitants by granting them special privileges in the fields of taxation and administration. He also strengthened the position of the local metropolitan bishop. As a result, the city passed peacefully into Turkish control, while the Sultan's troops were able to loot and ravish the surrounding countryside.

Six years later, the Athenians conspired with Franco Acciaioli to rid themselves of the Turks and 'the Conqueror' came back, waging ruthless war and exiling ten noble families. The first period of Turkish rule was marked by natural disasters, epidemics and pirate raids. Yet the city and its people held on bravely in adverse circumstances, and the traveller Curtius was still able to note that "the city has orchards, many olives, and citrus trees - bitter oranges and lemons".

BETWEEN THE SCYLLA OF THE TURKS TO THE CHARYBDIS OF VENICE

In September 1687, just as the Athenians were beginning to recover from the blows of nature and their fellow-men, their city was placed under siege by the Venetian forces of Francesco Morosini. Morosini set up four batteries of cannon and bombarded the Acropolis for five days without respite, despite the fact that the Turks were using the Parthenon as a gunpowder store. Eventually, a Venetian cannonball landed inside the temple and blew a huge hole in one of the most perfect of man's creations.

Morosini occupied Athens for five months, a time filled with looting and acts of barbarism. But in March 1688, the future Doge and his army retreated, judging that they could no longer hold the castle of Athens. They took with them as many marble lions and other works of art as they could, the first large-scale theft of art treasures in modern Greek history, and one committed with the blessing of the Most Serene Republic of Venice, which soon found itself adorned with some superb works of art. As Morosini withdrew in the face of the vengeful Turks, he was accompanied by the populace of Athens. The city emptied for three whole years, during which time it was burned, raided and laid waste.

CHRONICLE OF A CITY ENSLAVED

In the spring of 1688 the Turkish-Venetian War came to an end and Athens was back in Ottoman hands. The Turks built a little mosque inside the battered Parthenon. Outside the 'castle' (the Acropolis), the city was fortified with the Serpentzes wall and the shorter wall of Ipapanti. As for the Athenians, they came home after three years and life returned to the city. Greek schools were opened, and for all the epidemics, natural disasters and famines, the Greek population managed to survive. And as the city and its people were pulling themselves together, the first wave of foreign visitors arrived, some, but not all of them, drawn by their love of the ancient world. Athens had become a small but cosmopolitan town, with a population of 10,000 souls, 300 churches, five mosques, five Turkish baths, and 16 fountains. Above it loomed the rugged rock on which the 'castle' stood, and all around lay wonderful ruins which had endured the tests of time and human barbarity. The finishing touch to the picture of the town at this time was provided by the slim minarets whose perpendicular lines set off the masses of the buildings and the occasional curves of church domes.

In the second half of the 18th century, the fortune-hunters of Europe set their sights on Athens. In 1751, the British Association of Dilettanti sent out the architects Stuart and Revett to survey the ancient monuments, and at about the same time the German intellectual Winckelmann inaugurated the Classical movement. Athens was to become a source of inspiration once more, and from the darkness of its slavery was to dispatch a message of light to the West.

ATHENS BECOMES THE MALIKIANES OF HASEKIS

"1760, in that year Athens became a malikianes [geographical region] belonging to the Sultan and leased out for the duration of the lessee's lifetime. The purchaser of the lease had administrative rights over the inhabitants of the land...". In 1772, Haji Ali Hasekis (the name means 'bodyguard') became lessee of the land, and he plunged the Athenians into fresh misadventures: "it was decided to build a wall a-round the city and this was done in three months, with the help of all the city and the villages and the Muslims as well. The whole work was finished, and the city was secured with five gates, the Albanian Gate or Plaka Gate to the south, the Mesoyeia Gate to the east, the Gate of the Holy Apostles to the north, the Gate of the Gypsies to the north-west and the fifth, the Mandravilis Gate, to the south-west. There was another gate on the Acropolis" (extracts from the memoirs of P. Skouzes). To these gates we should add another, the Arch of Hadrian, now called the 'Arched Door of the Princess'. In fact, the wall was not intended for defensive use, but to allow Hasekis to exert complete control over the Athenians, upon whom he had already imposed harsh taxation combined with public whippings and other humiliations. In 1795, this brutal governor, under whom the Athenians had suffe-red as never before, was beheaded on the orders of the Sultan. "Because of the tyranny of Haji Ali, three fifths of the Athenians left the city, going east, or to the islands, or to the nearby villages" (Skouzes). The early nineteenth century was also marred by the looting of the Parthenon, the Acropolis and the other Athenian monuments. Lord Elgin, Louis Fauvel, and other foreigners —some of their names have come down to us, others not— took advantage of the circumstances and, in the name of a 'love' of Greek antiquities, bore off many of the immortal works still to be found in the city. Fortunately, however, there were among the foreigners nu-merous Philhellenes —the names of Chateaubriand, Eynard and Byron come to mind— who did much to help the Greeks in their struggle for liberty.

THE FIRST SWALLOWS IN ATHENS

The Athenians, fully aware of their great historical responsibilities, were prepar-ing for the national uprising. Three heroic elders of the town, Angelos Yerontas, Prokopios and Palaiologos Benizelos, had become members of the revolutionary organisation called the Society of Friends, and had spread its ideas through the

Attic countryside. With great secrecy, they assembled the necessary weapons and readied themselves. On 25 March 1821, when the War of independence broke out in the rest of Greece, the elders offered themselves as hostages in a move planned to reassure the Turks. At dawn on 25 April, the Athenians stormed the Acropolis and settled down to a siege of it that was to last 13 months. It was not until 10 June 1822 that the first siege was over, and the Turks were compelled to hand over the keys. After centuries of slavery, the Acropolis, the monument that symbolises all Greece, was once more in the hands of the Athenians, the Greeks.

After this came four productive years in which much progress was made. But the intoxication of victory had hardly worn off before trouble began among the ranks of the freedom-fighters and the politicians. Selfishness and a liking for power have been faults that have tormented the proud soul of the Greeks since ancient times, and still do so today.

"THE SUN HAS SET AND THE MOON HAS VANISHED"

In July 1826, the Turks returned, in greater force. Hostilities began again, and dragged on for months. As the fighting in the town grew fiercer, the women and children took once more to the roads as refugees. The street-fighting which followed laid waste much of Athens and badly damaged many of the monuments.

The atmosphere in the castle, under siege for nearly a year, was gloomy. As evening fell and the May moon rose, sad but beloved music welled up like a requiem for free Athens. The voice of the singer, accompanying himself on the long-necked lute, rent the air and the hearts of those who heard him:

The sun has set, O Greeks, and the moon has vanished.

Just a few days later, on 25 May 1827, the crimson crescent moon flew once more in the Athenian sky. The cost in blood had been a heavy one: the city had more than 1,500 dead to mourn (a quarter of the pre-war Greek population) and ten Philhellenes, seven of them French, two Spanish and one Genoese.

THE SECOND SIEGE OF THE ACROPOLIS; the thoughts of Makriyannis, illustrated by the hand of D. Zografos (Benaki Museum).

"The eternal Greek, with all his virtues and all his faults, has made history down the millennia-history based upon universal principles... And he made that history as he felt it in his bones, with elation, with obstinacy and with dissension. If he had not done it that way, what sort of Greek would he have been?" (Dimitrios A. Yerontas).

The fact that they had recaptured the castle was of little help to the Turks. The Ottoman Empire was tottering, and its continued presence in Greece was a lost cause. The Great Powers, seeing the damage being done to trade in the Middle East and the growing tide of public opinion in favour of Greece, switched sides and decided to impose a truce and arrange matters so as to benefit the former slaves of the Turks. In July 1827, Britain, France and Russia signed the Treaty of London, by which Greece was officially recognised as a "semi-independent state".

The Greeks were lucky in their first governor, the great statesman Ioannis Capodistrias. A political figure of international standing, Capodistrias was an early proponent of European unification, supported the emancipation of the blacks, drew up the constitution of Switzerland (where he is still honoured as a national benefactor), made peace in Poland and protected the interests of France after the defeat of Napoleon. In 1828, he resigned from his post as Foreign Minister of Russia and came to Greece with the vision of serving his tormented homeland. He negotiated the withdrawal of Ibrahim's troops from the Peloponnese, and masterminded the recapture of Central Greece. But perhaps his greatest triumph was the London Protocol of 1830, by which the independence of the Greek state was recognised.

The progress that Greece was making came to an abrupt halt in September 1831, when Capodistrias was assassinated. The governments of Britain and France were morally responsible for the deed: it was they who placed the weapons in the hands of the Mavromichalis family, who performed the act. The Greek state, taking its first hesitant steps, had stumbled into chaos.

THE COMING OF THE SPRING

The spring of 1830 was among the most joyful in the modern history of the Athenians. Now they were free to return home, but there were some unpleasant surprises awaiting them, as the majority of their houses were no more than heaps of ruins. Reconstruction began, and everyone struggled to set the city on its feet.

The majority of the Turks sadly left the soil of Attica, and returned to the Asian lands whence they had come.

In February 1832, the Great Powers decided that monarchy was the future of Greece, and they appointed Othon, son of the Philhellene King Ludwig of Bavaria, as the first King of Greece. In January 1833, the Greeks accorded him an enthusiastic reception when he arrived at Nafplio. The 17 year-old Bavarian prince was accompanied by four (Bavarian) regents who were to govern until he came of age. The regents spoke no Greek and knew nothing of the local mentality or conditions. Their laws were harsh, and they treated slightlingly those who had fought for the freedom of Greece. Othon himself, however, was popular: he learned flawless Greek and much of the country's history, travelling the land and getting to know his people. At that time, Nafplio was the provisional capital of Greece, and the country ran no further north than a line from Arta in Epirus to Lamia on the southern boundaries of Thessaly. In Athens, the ruins were coming to life. On 31 March 1833 a Bavarian garrison took over from the Turks on the Acropolis. The Turkish houses on the Sacred Rock filled up with happy Bavarians, and the blue-and-white Greek flag flew proudly in the sky of Athens.

ATHENS AS CAPITAL
September 1834 was a time of 'congratulations from Nafplio', as Athens was proclaimed capital of the newly-formed Greek state. King Othon installed himself in the Kontostavlos mansion, while the 2,000 civil servants filled to overflowing the few buildings of any size in the city.

Now Athens resembled the phoenix rising from the ashes, with fine houses in the neo-Classical style rising from the ruins of the Turkish town. The architects Kleanthes and Schaubert had already prepared the first town plan, which made provision for the city to expand in a northerly direction, for wide streets and for plenty of parks. Although the plan received official approval, it encountered vociferous opposition from the owners of land who stood to lose by its implementation. In the summer of 1834, King Ludwig sent the architect Leo von Klenze to draw up a new plan, but this proved to be a much less inspired conception. As the scholar Costas Biris, an expert on Athens, remarks, "instead of a city capable of development and growth, as Kleanthes had seen the question of Athens, von Klenze's city was enclosed and monolithic". Today, as the twenty-first century approaches, the Athenians are still suffering the consequences of the implementation of Klenze's plan.

In June 1835, Othon came of age, and everyone expected him to dispense with the services of his regents. But one of them, Armansperg, was appointed prime minister and, in effect, ruled Greece. In 1836 the foundations of the royal palace were laid, and in the autumn Othon married his bride Amalia. When the spring of 1837 came, the Athenians acquired the university for which they had longed, and over the next four years the city was adorned with some magnificent buildings in the Classical style then at the height of its influence.

THE RISING OF 3 SEPTEMBER - THE FIRST CONSTITUTION

"It was not money and property that I wanted, but a constitution for my country so that it could be ruled by laws and not highhandedly", trumpeted General Makriyannis in 1843. His voice was one in a swelling chorus of protest as the Greeks determined that change must come. On the evening of 2 September 1843, a huge demonstration filled the square in front of the palace, and achieved its purpose: on the following day it was announced that Greece was to be given a constitution. In commemoration of that great day, the main square of the city, once the Garden of the Muses, later backed by the Palace (now Parliament), was called Constitution Square (*Syntagma*).

On 3 September 1843 Greece had a chance to be reborn. There was a widespread feeling that the mistakes of the past should be forgotten. King Othon was

"Othon was a dreamer. He made the Great Idea his own cause. His political failings drove him out, but his towering spiritual virtues kept him in the memory of the Greek people. He was just a visitor to Athens, on his way from Munich to Byzantium" (Zacharias Papantoniou).

popular with the Greeks. He had learned a love of the country from his Philhellene father Ludwig, who had instilled in him the vision of the 'Great Idea' the reconquering, that is, of all the lands which had once been Greek and their reunification in a state with Constantinople as its capital. Othon spoke excellent Greek and never wore anything but Greek national dress. His prestige rose still further when he stoutly opposed the blockade imposed on Piraeus by the British fleet in the winter of 1850. His patriotism impressed his subjects during the Crimean War, when he fell out with the Greek government over his belief that the conflict provided an opportunity for Greece to move against the Turks. During Othon's thirty-year reign, modern Greek arts and letters flourished.

As the years went by, however, the political atmosphere became rather more gloomy and the people, deprived of real democratic freedoms, had to deal also with harsh economic conditions. In middle age, Othon became suspicious and autocratic and the fact that there was no heir to the throne made the situation more difficult still. The so-called 'Herculeses of the Crown' (cronies of the monarch) led Othon (ever a dreamer) into confrontations with the students of Athens (a ridiculous squabble over imported straw hats) and with the progressives (over attempts to amend the constitution). The Great Powers were no better pleased with Othon, who had become reluctant to serve their interests, and so it was decided to remove him. On 12 October 1862, Othon and Amalia left Greece, with tears in their eyes. Five years later, Othon died in Bavaria and was buried, by his wish, wearing the Greek *'fustanella'*.

After the deposition of Othon, the prime minister spoke to a meeting in 'Othonos Square': "Let us swear in the name of this square, now fittingly renamed Omonia Square, [Concord: then as now] that we will be faithful to our country and obedient to the patriotic decisions taken". Concord was, however, the last feeling that could be described as dominant in Greece, and the Athenians were divided into two rival factions, the 'mountain party' and the 'plains party'. Coup followed coup and plot succeeded plot, culminating in the 'June incident' when Omonia Square and the streets around it became a battle field.

THE SECOND MONARCHY - THE ROYAL REPUBLIC

The depressing events of 1863 and the chaotic situation in the country were a source of great concern to the Athenians, who felt the need of a leader. The Great Powers, too, were searching for a monarch who was well-disposed towards them and who would be prepared to involve himself in Greek affairs without making any unreasonable demands. Eventually, the choice fell upon Prince William George of Denmark, who arrived in Greece in 1863. King George I, as he became, was welcome because he brought with him a British commitment to unite the Ionian Islands with Greece; in fact, this move was advantageous to Britain, who rid herself of an area which was constantly in revolt, while at the same time acquiring a considerable degree of influence over the King.

The first months of George's reign were not much of a honeymoon because of discontent over the absolutist ways of his adviser, Count Sponneck. A protest meeting in Omonia Square on 30 October 1865 showed the strength of Athenian feeling against the Count, who was compelled to return to Denmark just a few months later. Athens, in the meantime, was growing more beautiful with each passing day; the tasteful neo-Classical houses were becoming more numerous and proving the city worthy of its exalted historical and intellectual past, just as Ludwig of Bavaria had envisaged. The population was growing, too, and had reached almost 40,000. These people were a human mosaic in a typical Greek style, with all the differences blending into a general uniformity in which everyone was first and foremost a citizen of Athens.

In 1863, the 2nd National Assembly met to adopt a new constitution, a process which dragged on and on because of difficulties with the progressive deputies from the Ionian Islands. The Greeks ultimately acquired a 'royal republican' system of government, but there was plenty of scope for the king to intervene in politics, and this successive monarchs frequently did. Between this time and 1875 there were repeated changes of government, with the conservatives and the 'democrats' alternating in power. The most significant political personality of the time, however, was Alexandros Koumoundouros, under whose prime ministership the economy improved, trade grew and the middle classes and the farmers enjoyed better conditions. The idea of liberating Crete and Thessaly gained support at this time. Koumoundouros was followed by the charismatic Charilaos Trikoupis, who in 1874 wrote a newspaper article entitled 'Who is to Blame?' accusing the King of meddling in politics and proposing that governments should be able to demonstrate that they enjoyed the support of parliament.

The economic recovery led to an upsurge in building. Athens gained numerous magnificent buildings in the neo-Classical style in which great architects had displayed the full range of their talents. In 1876, the Stock Exchange opened, and money flowed into the country from Greeks in communities abroad who benefited from the generous facilities provided by the government and who sometimes became, in turn, national benefactors. War between Russia and Turkey broke out in 1877, but Trikoupis and George I agreed that Greece should keep her distance from the belligerents, thus passing up an opportunity to expand the country's borders. In 1881, however (when Koumoundouros was prime minister again), Thessaly and Arta in Epirus were annexed. Progress continued, along with work on major public projects: railways, gas, water supply, electric lighting. In 1888 the Athens Municipal Theatre was opened; paid for out of a gift from Andreas Syngros, it was designed by Ziller. Sculpture and painting flourished, too. The best-known painters of the time are Nikiforos Lytras, Nikolaos Ghyzis and Yeorgios Iakovidis, while among the sculptors the name of Yannoulis Halepas stands out.

THE ANCIENT AGORA.
Here, beneath the bridge, the "sweet, honeyed, gentle and intoxicating song" sent soaring out on the evening breeze by the flute of the last Dervish was heard for the last time. Papadiamandis, who lived nearby, was wakened by the melody and the words of the Muslim in his decline: "The world is a wheel, and it turns". Then the Dervish and his flute vanished into the magic of the night, and were never heard of again. 'Athens, city of the East', was no more.

Athens University developed into a channel for ideological and political trends, and had more students than any other university in Europe. In 1896 the Olympic Games were revived in the Panathenaic Stadium, and Spyros Loues won the very first modern Marathon race. In politics, instability was the order of the day, with frequent changes of government, a two-party system and an ever-growing number of civil servants. Whenever the government changed, all the civil servants appointed by the previous government were dismissed so that those favoured by its successor could be appointed. In a newspaper article, the Athens scholar Kambouroglou named the square where the dismissed civil servants had the habit of gathering "the garden of tears", and thus accidentally gave the area the name it still bears today: Klafthmonos Square. Life could have been pleasant in late 19th-century Athens, but for the protracted political and economic crisis caused by the insistence of Trikoupis on implementing an economic policy which favoured only the capitalists and harmed the middle and lower middle classes. On 10 December 1893, Trikoupis was forced to declare the state officially bankrupt. Two years later, after an electoral defeat, he left for Paris, where he died in 1896. Crete rose in revolt against the Turks once again in 1897 and Greece, unaided, was forced into war with Turkey, a war which she lost and she had to accept international economic control. Britain was prepared to offer Crete autonomy, under the sovereignty of the Sultan. The borders in Thessaly were adjusted to the benefit of Turkey, and the vision of the Great Idea seemed to be lost forever. Against this background, the capital continued to grow, reaching a population of 100,000.

THE ALMOND TREES BLOSSOM

As the 20th century dawned, the atmosphere in the capital was one of protracted winter. Athens was (and still is) a city divided against itself, with a population that appears to belong to two different societies. On the one hand was the flourishing, 'neo-Classical', quasi-European set, with a vigorous 'high society' and much cultural life. And on the other was the 'backward' majority of the ordinary people, who belonged to a society of a markedly Mediterranean nature.

The Classicism of Athens acquired a degree of French elegance at this time, with fine examples of eclecticism and Art Nouveau, but neo-Baroque tended to predominate and the new buildings lacked the imposing severity of their predecessors. In the world of the theatre, the early 20th century saw the foundation of two organisations which were aware of current thinking in the world of the arts and attempted to introduce repertory theatre. These organisations were the Royal Theatre of Thomas Economou, with Marika Kotopouli as its principal actress, and the New Theatre of Constantinos Christomanos, with Kyveli as its star.

By 1908, the population of Athens was 175,000 and living conditions had much improved. But the threat of war hung over the heads of all, like the sword of Damocles. Macedonia, still Turkish-occupied, was a simmering cauldron, and in 1904 the heroic death there of the Greek freedom-fighter Pavlos Melas had sent a shock through the entire Greek world and underscored the significance of what was called the 'Macedonian struggle'. The only good news was from Crete, when as Eleftherios Venizelos announced "as of yesterday [15 July 1908], for the first time after seven whole centuries since Crete fell to the Venetians, there is not one single foreign soldier upon Cretan soil".

At this time, Macedonia was the scene of the Young Turk rising. Although they claimed to be progressives, the aim of the Young Turks was "to make the Greeks into law-abiding Ottoman citizens". And on 15 August 1909, a group of 500 patriots, many of them veterans of the fighting in Macedonia and all of them members of the Military League, rebelled at the Goudi army camp in Athens, demanding the reorganisation of the army. This was, perhaps, the only military coup which benefited Greece rather than damaging it. Since the revolutionaries found none of the leaders of the old parties to their liking, they turned in their search for "a person capable of expressing [their] purpose of revitalisation" to Crete, and the distinguished politician Eleftherios Venizelos.

ATHENS AT WAR

The Balkan Wars broke out in 1912. The military victories of the Greek Army (led by Crown Prince Constantine) and the diplomatic triumphs of Venizelos embodied in the Treaties of London (May 1913) and Bucharest (August 1913) doubled the geographical size of Greece. The Greek flag now flew over Epirus, Macedonia and the islands of the eastern Aegean. The Athenians of the Belle Epoque knew they were living in historic times.

After the First World War, Venizelos succeeded in the Treaties of Neuilly (1919) and Sèvres (1920) in gaining for Greece the European side of the Dardanelles, sovereign rights over the Aegean islands, and the administration of the vilayet of Smyrna in Asia Minor. The country thus doubled in size, its relations with its neighbours improved, and its international prestige reached new heights. Despite the cruelties of war, this was a period of great euphoria in Greece. Literature flourished, and the 'literary salons' of Athens sparkled. In the visual arts, the forerunners of what was called the 'Generation of the Thirties' appeared. In the theatre, this was the golden age of the revue, and light opera was very popular.

Unfortunately, however, the confused and unco-ordinated manner in which the subsequent military campaigns in Asia Minor were conducted, the stout resistance of the Turks, and a shift in Allied policy combined to bring about the tragedy of 1922. The Great Powers looked the other way as the Turks massacred and robbed the Greek population of Asia Minor. The thoughtless advance on Ankara cost the Greeks a million dead and one and a half million refugees. When the refugees began to flood into Athens, the population of the capital more than doubled and the city had to cope with almost insuperable problems.

In 1923, the Lausanne Conference decided that there would be a compulsory exchange of minorities between Greece and Turkey. Pacts with Italy (in 1928) and Turkey (1930) did much to restore Greece's position, and in domestic affairs Venizelos continued his far-sighted work. Agriculture progressed, laws to protect workers were passed, and top priority was given to settling the refugees. Athens began to spread out, and suburbs appeared. The problem of the city's water supply was solved by the reservoir constructed at Marathonas, the public transport system was improved and the entire city was electrified. Important advances were made in education, too, with the construction of new schools and the introduction for the first time of the vernacular language into secondary education. The Generation of the '30s, with its messages about a return to 'Greekness', to the roots and values of the Greek nation, gave a fresh impetus to the arts and letters.

Venizelos died in March 1936, depriving Greece at a crucial moment in her history of a great political figure who had pushed the borders of Greece from Thessaly to cover two continents and five different seas. Pavlos Nirvanas said of Venizelos that he had in his soul "the grain of mustard seed that can move the mountains built by God", and that he was "the man who believed in the eternal miracle, the miracle of his nation". An ambiguous situation ensued, with the return, in the person of George II, of the monarchy (which had been abolished after the Asia Minor fiasco). On 4 August 1936, the monarch and Ioannis Metaxas, his prime minister, established a personal dictatorship. Britain supported the Fascist regime in Greece, whose actual allegiance was to Hitler's Germany. Under Metaxas, intellectual activity was controlled and censorship was imposed, but, as is often the case with totalitarian regimes, the fine arts were looked on with much greater favour.

On 28 October 1941, war broke out with Fascist Italy. In April 1941, the Germans attacked Greece for the purpose, according to the Third Reich, of driving the British forces out of the country. The Greek generals, faced with war on two fronts, were compelled to surrender, and at dawn on 27 April 1941 Hitler's army entered Athens and paraded through the empty streets. The Athenians stayed at home: resistance to the invader had begun. Before long, Italian forces arrived, and Athens came under dual occupation. Now a fresh and tragic period began for the Athenians. The occupying forces soon ran through such stocks as there were of food, fuel and other commodities. The population of Athens died of hunger in droves. Emaciated corpses soon became a common sight on the streets. Hunger and want were matched only by the mass torturing and execution of Greek patriots. The SS detention centres in Merlin and Korai Sts and the Kaisariani Rifle Range became places of sacrifice. The national resistance movement consisted of the movements ELAS-EPON and OPLA (representing the Communist Left) and EDES and EKKA (whose members were drawn from the Right). Churchill, impressed by the bravery of the Greeks, remarked in the Commons that henceforth we should say not that the Greeks fought like heroes, but that heroes fight like the Greeks.

On 12 October 1944, the retreating Germans left Attica and the streets of Athens filled with the citizens of the capital celebrating their liberation. The outburst of joy lasted six days, and culminated in the arrival of the government-in-exile and a speech by prime minister George Papandeou in Syntagma Square. Unfortunately, however, the various factions of what had been the resistance movement came under the influence of other countries and were drawn into conflict and, ultimately, a tragic civil war.

In the summer of 1944, Churchill and Stalin had signed an agreement (which even Churchill admitted was cynical and makeshift) by which put Greece in the Western sphere of influence. The agreement was kept secret for many years; but historians today believe that if the political forces of Greece had been informed officially, and in good time, of its content the civil war might have been averted.

LIBERATION: the flag is raised on the Acropolis by George Papandreou, 12 October 1944
(National Historical Museum).
"Wherever you stand, this is sacred ground. A curse upon those that defile it, whether they be foreigners or traitors. Nemesis is merciless. The justice of God unfolds like the Second Coming. On this day, the tears and the cares of the prisoners, of the dead and of the other sad Greeks are transformed into achievement, into wild joy. On this day, the Greeks, like lovers, become one with their country" (Ioanna Tsatsou).

ATHENS TODAY

The Fifties proved to be a fateful decade for the appearance of the capital. The population of Athens almost doubled, with people from the provinces abandoning the 'scorched earth' that the civil war had left behind it and flooding into the capital in search of work. The needs of the population and a profiteering mentality, helped to mould human behaviour and the environment. Even the buildings of Athens were affected; the neo-Classical houses, with their wrought-iron balconies and tiled roofs, were turned over to the tender mercies of the bulldozers. In their place rose faceless structures whose harsh geometric lines contaminated and humiliated the landscape of Attica. Monsters worse than any Homer could have imagined ravaged the land, turning Athens into a bloated cement jungle that is 'home' to four million people. But, the Athenians came to realise the ugliness of their city and to set about taking action. Monuments are being restored now, the new pedestrian precincts and little parks are oases of green with a message of optimism, and the number of lovers of Athens has once again begun to grow. Even in the aesthetic poverty of recent decades, the shade of the Parthenon never ceased to fall on values which survived unpolluted.

There are still brilliant days when the clarity of the atmosphere overcomes the smog, illuminating the monuments and people's faces alike. There are friendly people, Mediterranean in temperament and Greeks to the marrow, happiest when seated at table by the hearth of the family with its powerful bonds. There are still countless admirers of Dionysus and Terpsichore, and their cheerful bands fill the tavernas. There are theatres, scores of theatres, and cultural events —places where actors and audience can meet. The streets hum with life day and night. When evening falls and the moon is high, the floodlit monuments emit an irresistable appeal, crying out to be strolled around. By night or by day, Athens has allure. On its sacred rock, the Acropolis, all the deities of the earth still protect it. This is a place of the gods, a place of magic.

"ATHENS, 1971", *(Spyros Vassilíou).*

AN EVENING IN ATHENS, water-colour, I. Rizos, 1897 (National Gallery, Athens).

THE MONUMENTS OF ATHENS

I. THE ACROPOLIS: A PLACE OF PILGRIMAGE FOR LOVERS OF BEAUTY

The word acropolis comes from two Greek roots: *akron*, meaning a high place, and polis, meaning a town or city. The 'highest place of the town' was used as a fortress, a place where one was safe, the first place where the city had been and, thus (metaphorically), a place worth defending. When written with a capital A (in Greek and in most of the world's other languages), it refers specifically to the Acropolis of Athens, the most famous acropolis, the place where Western civilisation came to birth.

I.1 The Propylaea

In 437 BC, the Athenians chose Mnesicles as the architect of the Propylaea. He gave the entrance to the Sacred Rock the monumental character most appropriate to it, enabling it to predispose the visitor and prepare him for the mental and spiritual uplift, the tremor of religious feeling that would run through him when he saw the Parthenon. The Propylaea of Mnesicles, then, was an invitation to the visitor.

The earliest propylon ('before the gate' i.e., entrance) to the prehistoric Acropolis was built in Mycenaean times. Much later, under the tyranny, the Pisistratids constructed a limestone propylon in the Archaic style. The third propylon was the pre-Classical one built immediately after the unexpected victory at Marathon, and was probably destroyed when the Persians devastated Athens ten years later. The fourth is the structure we admire today, and it dates from the time of Pericles.

THE ACROPOLIS IN THE 2ND CENTURY A. D.

117. So-called Ergasterion
118. Shrine of Zeus Polieus
119. Temple of Rome and Augustus
120. Parthenon
121. Altar of Athena
122. Erechtheum
123. Pandroseum
124. The Arrephoreum
125. Athena Promachos
126. Chalkotheke
127. Artemis Brauronia
128. Propylaea
129. Temple of Athena Nike
130. Agrippa Monument
131. Beulé Gate
132. Panathenaic Way
133. Clepsydra
134. Apollo Hypoacraeus

135. Cave of Pan
136. Cave of Aglaurus
137. Shrine of Eros and Aphrodite
138. Peripatus Inscription
139. Odeum of Pericles
140. Temple of Dionysus
141. Theatre of Dionysus
142. Thrasyllus Monument
143. Nicias Monument
144. Stoa of Eumenes
145. Asclepieum
146. Ionic stoa
147. Odeum of Herodes Atticus
148. Shrine of Nymphe

(I. Travlos)

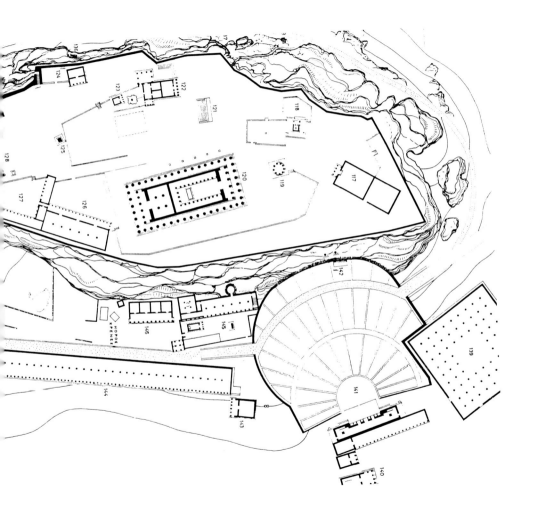

The Propylaea of Mnesicles consists of three 'wings'. The central and largest section contains five gates, and to the right and left are wings on an asymmetrical floor plan. A plain, severe Doric style is used for the external columns of the Propylaea, while inside, to the right and left of the entrance, are colonnades in the Ionic style. It was an Athenian custom to combine the Doric and Ionic, and the city's craftsmen were experts in doing so in such a way as to maintain an aesthetic balance. The Propylaea was the last building in the programme devised by Pericles, since the site was used first to store the building materials for the other temples. When the rest of the work on the Sacred Rock was complete, the monumental gateway was laid out and Mnesicles' architectural creation began to rise - but was never completed, since the Peloponnesian War which broke out in 431 BC brought everything to an abrupt standstill. That is why here and there in the outer walls we can still see the protrusions in the marble that were used to anchor the ropes by which the blocks of marble were raised into position. The protrusions would have been removed by the masons when the building was completed, which of course they did not have time to do on all the walls of the Propylaea.

The north wing of the Propylaea (to the left of the entrance) is called the Pinakotheke (art gallery). We are told by the traveller Pausanias (mid-second century AD) that this was a "building with pictures"; that is, it contained paintings showing the heroes of Homer, Alcibiades at the Nemean Games and other figures, created by the famous painter Polygnotus. Needless to say, this was not a museum of painting in the sense of a modern art gallery, given that the paintings were votive offerings to the goddess. The symmetry of the south wing had to be sacrificed to the sanctity of earlier buildings which encroached on the site which Mnesicles had hoped would be entirely devoted to his Propylaea (part of the sanctuary of Athena Nike and a section of Pelasgian wall).

In Byzantine times, the Propylaea became an episcopal palace, with a small chapel that may have been dedicated to the Archangels. The building acquired a roof, and took on the character of a fortress. The 'Franks', Catalans and Florentines who followed the Byzantines arranged their palaces inside and around the Propylaea, and the chapel became a Catholic church dedicated to St Bartholomew.

The tribulations of Athens and the Acropolis did not end there, however. When the Turks arrived, they took over the luxurious quarters in the Propylaea as the residence of the garrison commander, and the Pinakotheke was used as a powder magazine. There is a folk tale which connects the use of the building for this purpose with the church of St Demetrius 'Lumbardiaris' on the Hill of the Pnyx, nearby: on St Demetrius' day (26 October) 1648, it occurred to the Turks to shell the church from the Propylaea, aiming also at the congregation who had assembled to honour the saint on his feast-day. It would seem -according to the legend- that the shade of Mnesicles arose from the Elysian Fields and formed an alliance with St Demetrius, the warrior-saint. Together, they borrowed a thunderbolt from Zeus, lord of storms, and hurled it into the Turkish powder magazine. The explosion damaged the Propylaea and killed many of the inhabitants of the 'castle', including its 'High Aga', the Disdar Yusuf Aga. This is how the church of St Demetrius came by its nickname, which is a corruption of 'the Bombardier'. After the dreadful explosion, the Turks erected a tower -the Goulas or Koulas- at the SW corner of the Propylaea and used it as a prison. The Goulas was demolished in 1874 at the expense of Heinrich Schliemann.

At a lower level, in front of the Propylaea, stands the Beulé Gate named after the distinguished French archaeologist who excavated it in 1850). This was the entrance constructed towards the end of antiquity using building materials brought from the Choregic Monument of Nicias on the south slope of the Acropolis.

As we ascend towards the Propylaea, we come to a massive, high plinth in front of the Pinakotheke. On it originally stood a four-horse chariot group depicting

King Eumenes II of Pergamum (178 BC), erected to mark the king's contribution to the city of the famous Stoa of Eumenes. A century and a half later, the same monument was rededicated to Agrippa when he built the Odeum that stands in the Agora. We know there were many votive statues in the vicinity of the Propylaea, including a Hermes Propylaeus of Alcamenes, the Three Graces, a bronze lioness symbolising the girlfriend of the tyrannocide Aristogeiton, the Aphrodite of Calames and a bronze statue of Athena Hygeia, only the base of which has survived.

I.2 The Temple of Athena Nike

This delightful little temple stands on top of a bastion which is an outcrop of the strong Pelasgian wall. The position was an ideal one for defence, since any assailant would have to climb up with his right side -unprotected by his shield- turned towards the bastion. That perhaps explains why the top of the bastion was chosen as the place for the worship of the winged goddess Nike (victory), since there the defensive triumph was surely hers. Over the centuries, the prehistoric deity Nike gave way to the goddess Athena, becoming her servant and one of the properties or epithets of the city's patron.

In prehistoric times, the top of the bastion was occupied by a primitive altar on to which the devotees of the cult cast offerings to the dead and figurines depicting the deity being worshipped. Towards the end of the Archaic period, a small temple with an altar was erected on the same site, but this was destroyed by the Persians. In the time of Pericles, the Athenians faced the rock with limestone in such a way as to increase the height and width of the original bastion, on which the beautiful temple of Athena Nike was built a few years later. Its architect was Callicrates, known to us from his work on the Parthenon, and he seems to have used the plans for the earlier temple of Artemis Agrotera. Work on the temple began in 447 BC but took twenty years to complete.

VICTORY FASTENING HER SANDAL
(Acropolis Museum).
"This youthful body, caressed by the
folds of her transparent garment as
though by a lover's lips, is the most
perfect creation of Greek art. From
which azure or golden sky did this
ideal creation descend to be
respected even by time and kept
shining white? Could this nameless
Victory have been the Muse of
Phidias, who came to stand for one
more time on the Acropolis before
taking wing for ever?" (Gautier).

The temple is amphiprostyle, with four Ionic columns on the east side and four more on the west. The east frieze shows an assembly of the gods of Olympus, with Zeus, Athena and Poseidon in prominent positions, and there are scenes from the Persian wars on the other sides. The best sections of the frieze are in the British Museum, unfortunately, having been carried off by Lord Elgin. Inside the temple (in the cella, that is) was the Xoanon (wooden statue) of Athena, holding in her right hand a pomegranate, a symbol of fertility connected with the prehistoric deity Nike and demonstrating how that very ancient chthonic goddess continued to live on within Athena. Since the cult statue showed Athena, it was, of course, wingless, which was then explained as the wish of the Athenians that Victory should be unable to fly off to other cities.

Facing the temple is an impressive section of the Mycenaean wall which the ancient Greeks believed to have been constructed by the Pelasgians. Dating from the thirteenth century BC, it is as much as five metres thick and was built with just as much skill as the 'Cyclopean' walls of the same period to be found elsewhere in Mycenaean Greece. The platform on which the Temple of Athena Nike stands was surrounded by a parapet (415 BC) consisting of marble slabs ornamented with winged Victories. Among these superb sculptures, now to be admired in the Acropolis Museum, is the famous work depicting a Victory adjusting her sandal.

I.3 Statue of Athena Promachos

The visitor of ancient times, entering through the Propylaea, would have been faced by a tremendous sight: in front of him, on a number of levels, were several superb buildings surrounded by the countless works of art dedicated by pilgrims.

Among these works, a special place was occupied by the bronze statue of Athena Promachos, made by the great Phidias himself. The statue was dedicated by the Athenians after their victory at Marathon; it was nearly nine metres in height, and the goddess, standing upright with her spear and shield (Pausanias tells us that the shield was decorated with a scene from the Battle of the Centaurs, designed by the painter Parrasius and engraved by Mys) shone out with reflected light from high on the Acropolis rock.

I.4 Sanctuary of Artemis Brauronia

To the right of the Propylaea was the Sanctuary of Artemis founded in the mid-sixth century by Pisistratus, who brought the cult from his native town of Brauron. The Brauronion was an open-air sanctuary on whose south side colonnades formed a Greek, which was open to the Acropolis. In the colonnade were countless votive offerings, including most notably two impressive statues of the goddess: the old wooden statue (xoanon) brought from the seaside plain of Brauron, and a magnificent marble statue created by Praxiteles. Artemis Brauronia was the patroness of women before, during and after childbirth and of small children, and she retained her status as 'queen of the wild beasts', with the bear as her sacred animal. During the festival of the Lysizonia, young Athenian girls who were to wed made a symbolic dedication of their girdles at the Brauronion.

I.5 The Chalcotheke

Between the Brauronion and the Parthenon was a long, narrow colonnade, the Chalcotheke. This was where the priests kept the various bronze vessels and other valuable votive offerings.

I.6 The Erechtheum

This temple is the predominant feature on the north side of the Sacred Rock, and with its delicate harmony makes an ideal complement to the Doric perfection of the Parthenon.

Work on the Erechtheum began in 421 BC, after the peace of Nicias, and was not completed until 406 BC; the ongoing Peloponnesian War meant that construction took place by fits and starts. The Erechtheum is the most complex creation of Classical architecture, and its meaning spans a number of dimensions, given that its layout, its ornamentation and the cults honoured inside it are all greatly varied. In this way, the building is a symbol of the incredible variety of the Attic landscape and climate, and also of the beliefs of the free Athenians.

The Erechtheum, then, stands out for the freedom of its composition -a freedom which, however, obeys the harmonious concept of the building as a whole. The temple stands on uneven terrain, with its four sides on two different levels, yet the same roof covers a building where gods of the heaven and the underworld were worshipped together, along with heroes and symbols -all of them overshadowed by the figure of the great goddess, Athena Polias ('of the city').

The temple is divided into two parts. To the east is the Sanctuary of Athena Polias, a peaceful, rural deity with a very ancient 'heaven-sent' wooden cult statue (the ancient Greeks believed that the statue had fallen from heaven and had not been made by human hand - rather as some Christians believe of certain icons). During the Panathenaic Festival, the wooden statue was given a new robe which was placed on it by the maidens of the city. In the same part of the building was the famous gold lamp made by the sculptor Callimachus, which burned day and night and was so large it needed to be filled with oil only once a year. The west part of the Erechtheum was, perhaps, the most sacred, for it was here that the holy traces of the conflict between Poseidon and Athena were preserved. Here, too, Poseidon-Erechtheus was worshipped by the Athenians. Erechtheus was the mythical king of Athens who gave his name to the temple. In the Iliad, Homer tells us that Erechtheus was a son of Gaea (the Earth) whom Athena had taken into her temple and reared. The chthonic dimension of the figure of Erechtheus can be

THE ERECHTHEUM.
"This is one of the most fascinating peculiarities of sublime Greek art, which rarely took such liberties, and revitalised its established forms only with the ideal perfection of the detail. The entablature of the Pandrosium rests not on columns but on the Caryatids... The artist's inspiration for this idea must have come from watching the girls returning from the spring of Callirhoë with their urns carefully balanced on their heads... Lord Elgin took one of them away, and a copy has been put in her place" (Gautier).

seen in the etymology of his name. It would seem that Erechtheus was a primitive deity of the underworld who later became merged with Poseidon. When the cult of the Ionic deity Poseidon -god of earthquakes and the sea- came to Athens, Erechtheus yielded to him. It was said that in the Erechtheum was the chasm in the earth that was the tomb of Erechtheus, together with the tomb of Cecrops. Erechtheus and Cecrops are very likely the diverging developments of a single original figure, given that both were colonists and were worshipped as heroes and protectors of the city. With them was worshipped Boutes, brother of Erechtheus and another figure with connections with the underworld.

On the north-west side is an imposing porch leading to the interior of Poseidon's sanctuary. On the floor -once flooded with sea water- the signs of the god can still be seen: the chasm and the holes left by the three prongs of his trident. This was the famous sea called Erechtheos, whose waters, according to Pausanias, sounded like the waves of a real sea when the wind was in the south. Next, on the west side, is a humble olive tree, planted on the site of the ancient tree which was Athena's favourite symbol. In the underground depths of the Erechtheum lived the snake Erichthonius, a sacred creature which represented the spirit of Erechtheus. The priests of the temple made offerings of honey-cakes and milk to the snake. It is said that shortly before the Persian invasion the sacred snake disappeared and the offerings were left untouched, a sign to the Athenians that they, too, ought to leave their city because disaster was approaching.

The most striking part of the Erechtheum is the *porch of the Caryatids*, which stands above the Pandrosium, on the south-west side where the tomb of Cecrops is located. Each of the six lissom girls has a marble basket on her head, and also bears the weight of the roof. They may have symbolised the low position of women in Classical Athens. Later, they were called Caryatids, and their astounding beauty was the origin of an attractive story about their roots. After the Persian Wars, the story ran, the Athenians resolved to punish the people of Caryae in Laconia for having co-operated with the Persians. They invaded their country, captured their city and brought the women of Caryae -the Caryatids- back to Athens in slavery. Since the Caryatids were women of great beauty, the name came to be applied to any pretty girl, and so when the attractive statues went up on the Erechtheum it was only natural that they, too, should be called Caryatids. In the Christian era, the Erechtheum became a three-aisled basilica dedicated to Our Lady; under the 'Franks' it was a command post, and in Turkish times it was a harem. The Porch of the Caryatids is "one of the most fascinating peculiarities of high Greek art, which rarely took such liberties and confined itself to renewing established forms only in the ideal perfection of details" (Gautier).

I.7 The Arrephoreum

To the west of the Erechtheum stood a small and modest building called the Arrephoreum, which was the residence -briefly- of the Arrephorae, the girls who during a strange ceremony held every year as an echo of a local myth carried what were called the 'secret things'. These 'things' were contained in baskets covered with a length of cloth and were taken to the nearby sanctuary of Aphrodite in the Gardens, outside the north wall. There, the baskets were handed over to a priest and the girls were given fresh baskets which they brought back to the Arrephoreum to give to the priestess of Athena. The whole ceremony had to be carried out in complete secrecy by moonlight so as not to lose its power, and no one ever found out what was in the baskets. Lucian tells us that they contained miniature loaves of bread in the shape of snakes, phalluses, and the branches and cones of the umbrella pine, all symbols of fertility, but modern scholars incline to the view that the 'secret things' were no more than ordinary twigs on which the dew had settled. In places like Attica, the night dew was regarded as beneficial to fertility,

THE PROPYLEA.
"The luminous face and brilliant facade of the Acropolis"; "A triumphal ante-chamber, a colonnade which initiatives the thoughtful visitor and prepares him for the superhuman sight which awaits him as soon as he passes through its columns" (Gautier).

THE PARTHENON.
The offering of the state to Athena Parthenos, and a monument to Athenian politics. "This is an immortal lesson in consciousness and sincerity, where ideals have been crystallised in Pentelic marble" (Renan).

and so what could have been more valuable than the dew-drops which, as 'secret things', contributed to the continuing miracle of nature?

The Arrephorae were young girls aged from 7 to 11, and for a short time they lived in the Arrephoreum for the goddess's sake. The priestesses of the temple were also responsible for keeping the girls amused, which is why outside the Arrephoreum, to the west, was a small enclosed yard called the Ball-Court of the Arrephorae, where the girls could engage in various ball games.

I.8 The Archaic temple

In front of the Porch of the Caryatids, between the Erechtheum and the Parthenon, are the scanty traces of the temple built by the Pisistratids in 525 BC. The superb sculptures of the *Battle of the Giants* to be seen in the Acropolis Museum, the most perfect examples of Archaic pedimental carving, once belonged to this temple.

I.9 The rock-carved dedication

Near the Parthenon (26 metres from its north-west corner) is a Roman inscription carved into the rock. It reads: "Of Earth the fruit-bearer, in accordance with the oracle". On the small flat space it forms was a statue of Gaea (the Earth) which seemed to be emerging from the heart of the rock itself.

I.10 Sanctuary of Pandion

In the site now occupied by the basement of the Acropolis Museum was an ancient sanctuary to the hero Pandion, father of King Aegeus

I.11 Temple of Rome and Augustus

In Roman times, when Ares was Archon (27 BC), an elegant circular temple with nine Ionic columns was built directly in front of the Parthenon. It was dedicated to 'the goddess Rome and the god Augustus', and its Ionic columns were copies -or imitations- of the Classical Erechtheum.

I.12 Sanctuary of Zeus Polieus

At the highest point of the Sacred Rock, 156 metres above sea level, was the sanctuary of Zeus, here worshipped as 'Polieus' (protector of the city). The splendid altar was the focus of all the major rites held in Athens and, each June, of the Diopolia or Bouphonia ('ox-killing'). An ox was sacrificed after first being formally arraigned on a charge of impiety, thus removing the chance of a similar accusation being levelled at the priest who conducted the sacrifice. The sacrificed ox was an incarnation of the spirit of the vegetation of the previous year, which died with the harvest and yielded its place to the spirit of the new year.

I.13 The Parthenon

"The most perfect poem ever written in stone" (Lamartine) is a temple dedicated to Athena Parthenos, to "the purest creation of pagan mythology; springing from the head of Zeus fully grown and armed, she never bore a stain, not even that of birth" (Gautier).

At a meeting of the Ecclesia of the Deme (assembly) in 447 BC, the Athenians selected the experienced architects Ictinus and Callicrates to supervise the building of the temple and the eminent sculptor Phidias to decorate it. Fifty four artists —the best that the city could show— were set to work at top speed on the 'temple of temples'. On approximately the same site as the stereobate of the pre-Classical Parthenon, rose the Parthenon of the Golden Age. The temple was called the hecatompedon, the 'hundred-foot temple' a rather mysterious term. It may have been a reference to the interior length of the temple, or perhaps to the length of an earlier temple on the same site. The Parthenon has a number of architectural features which make it unique among temples in the Greek world. It is, first of all, the largest temple of Classical antiquity, laid out in the style known as peripteral with 8 columns on the short sides and 17 on the long. Although the order of the temple is primarily Doric, there are numerous Ionic elements, including the frieze and the columns. The *sekos* is amphiprostyle with eight columns, and consists of the cella and a west chamber. The cella is the 'box' in which the statue of the goddess was contained, and around it, like a "slow fossilised procession" marched the columns at a rhythmic pace. The colonnade stood out against the walls of the sekos, and the airy space between them reduces the mass of the building, which seems to float and almost to breathe. For that reason, the colonnade around the sekos was called the *pteron*, 'wing'.

The Parthenon is a vehicle for the intellectual virtues and democratic ideals of the Athenians of the Golden Age and has thus rightly been called a monument to Athenian policy. The relationship of dialogue to be observed on the Pnyx, when the Ecclesia of the Deme met and the minority respected the decision reached by the majority, is to be observed in every architectural detail of the monument: in the proportions of the columns, in the spaces between them, and in all the other parts of the temple, where the ratio of 4 to 9 is maintained.

The columns are noted for the features called *meiosis* and *entasis*. Meiosis is the way in which the column tapers as it rises, and entasis is the name given to the almost imperceptible swelling about 2/5 of the way up the column, where it has to thicken in order to bear the weight of the entablature. The great artists used these 'tricks' to give the marble life and movement and demonstrate its capacity to withstand weight. Such architectural details are called 'refinements', and they amount to a whole series of minor deviations from arid mathematical rigidity for the purpose of inspiring a pulse of life in the architectural creation.

The ancient Greeks went into these questions in depth. Aristotle went so far as to

THE PARTHENON in a coloured lithograph by Louis Dupré, Paris 1825.
"The most perfect poem in the world written in stone. Behind this symbol, the entire genius of the Greeks was offered up as a gift to the deity. Even ruinous, the Parthenon is a unique sight. Its sides are flushed golden by the veneer left by the sun as its rays touch the marble. This is the most sublime impression of ruins that ever emerged from human hand, because they are the ruins of the most beautiful work ever constructed in the world" (Lamartine).

note that in nature there are no such things as absolutely straight lines or perfect curves; only mathematicians can produce such shapes. Greek architecture discovered these geometric peculiarities at a very early date, and struggled to gain control over them and incorporate them into the architectural perfection of the Parthenon. In the course of their geometrical experiments, the architects of antiquity discovered that under the influence of the light, a straight line appears to be curved, and a curved line straight. In order to forestall this illusion, they constructed the Parthenon in such a way that all the horizontal lines are slightly curved. On the short sides of the temple, this convex curvature is 6 centimetres, and on the long sides it is 11; in other words, the stylobate (the platform on which the columns stand) is 6 and 11 cm. higher, respectively, in the centre than it is at the ends. This curvature extends downwards into the foundations of the temple.

The Parthenon is a building of controlled symmetry, of balancing opposites, just as is also the case in tragic poetry, in music, in the fine arts and in the democratic form of government. The columns stand on their apparently horizontal but actually slightly convex stylobate leaning gently inwards in a rather pyramidal manner. It has been calculated that the columns lean towards the centre of the temple as much as seven centimetres out of perpendicular, while in the four corners -where the columns are more massive because more light falls upon them- the inclination is as much as ten centimetres. If the columns did not come to an end at their capitals, they would converge 1,783 metres up in the air, forming a giant pyramid. Counterbalancing movements are thus tamed by contrasting tendencies, giving the Parthenon perfect balance and symmetry.

The interior of the cella is divided into three 'aisles' by two double colonnades. The middle 'aisle', which was the broadest, stretched up to the roof, while the side 'aisles' were divided into two storeys. A much shorter lateral colonnade joined the two longer ones, thus forming a Π shape. Directly in front of the lateral colonnade

FROM THE PARTHENON FRIEZE: POSEIDON, APOLLO AND ARTEMIS (Acropolis Museum)
"We feel that the chisel of Phidias must have trembled and burned in his hand when his
fingers were giving life to these sublime figures... That the artist was transfusing his own
personality, his very blood into the figures, into the veins of the creatures he was creating,
and that even today a part of his life pulsates in these living forms, in their members which
seem ready to move, into their lips which are ready to speak!" (Lamartine).

stood the gold and ivory ('chryselephantine') statue of Athena Parthenos, wrought by the great Phidias himself. The goddess, standing upright on a high plinth, held a Victory in her right hand and had her spear resting on her left shoulder. At her feet was her shield, with the Erichthonius snake. Pliny tells us the statue was 26 (Greek) feet high (about 12 metres). Thucydides relates that some 40 talents of gold were used to plate the imposing statue, a figure which Philochorus raises to 44 talents -that is, about 120 kilos of the precious metal. The shield and sandals of the virgin goddess were decorated, and there was a depiction of the Pandora myth on the plinth of the statue. Michael Choniates tells us that in the fifth century AD the statue was taken to Constantinople -after which it disappears from history. Today, such knowledge of its details as we have come from two poor Roman copies, the *Lenorman* and the *Varvakeio Athena*, which are in the Archaeological Museum.

The original purpose of the west chamber of the temple has not been fully identified. However, the Athenians used it for the safekeeping of the funds of the Athenian League, the Public Treasury, the money belonging to the goddess, and other precious relics such as the silver stool from which the Persian king Xerxes watched the battle of Salamis.

The external ornamentation of the temple was as follows. On the metopes of the east side was the Battle of the Giants, with the Battle of the Centaurs on the south, the Battle of the Amazons on the west and the Fall of Troy on the north. The east pediment is the earliest section of the decoration, and showed the birth of Athena. The central figures in this composition disappeared early in the Christian era, and probably fell victim to religious fanaticism. On the west pediment of the Parthenon, which is a later and technically more advanced composition, the visitors of ancient times would have marvelled at the conflict between Poseidon and Athena, conveyed in all its grandeur. The superb central figures were shattered when

Morosini attempted to detach them from the Parthenon and carry them off to Venice. The best-preserved pieces of the pediment adorn the British Museum today -a tribute to the mania for collection of Lord Elgin- while some fragments and a single group (possibly showing Cecrops and Pandrosus) are in the Acropolis Museum. The pedimental sculpture was in high relief, and is among the most magnificent creations of the human hand.

On the outer side, the wall of the sekos is ornamented with an incomparable Ionic frieze depicting the stately Panathenaic procession. Mortals and immortals, men and gods, march endlessly round the frieze, praising the city of Athens and hymning its democracy. The Parthenon frieze is a milestone in the history of art and human civilisation since in it, for the first -and perhaps the last- time, nobility of spirit combined with sublime artistic values to produce a collective work of unique perfection. Today, the Parthenon stands battered and naked, after its many misadventures (earthquakes, theft, conversion, fire), but still stubborn on its Sacred Rock, telling the tale of the great moments and the difficult hours in the history of Athens. This is a monument which is unique in every respect, even in its ruined state. Kambouroglou was quite right when he said, "If these ruins are ever restored, the Parthenon will no longer exist".

II. THE PERIPATUS

Peripatus was the name given by the ancient Greeks to the road that ran round the Acropolis. It had a total length of five stades and eight (Greek) feet -that is, 900-930 metres. The Acropolis rock is 156 feet high, and its top occupies an area of 15,000 square metres. It consists of Athenian limestone and schist, a rock formation also known as *kimilia*. Towards the top, the schist is hard and the water runs off it, while lower down there are considerable deposits of clay, which the water does not permeate and where wells can form. Erosion of these rock formations has created the caves which give the Sacred Rock something of its mystery, and the imaginative Athenians, influenced by the rugged rock and the wealth of their mythology, moulded tales of fairies and princesses about the recesses in the cliff faces.

II.1 The north slope of the Acropolis

The first ruins we come to on the ancient Peripatus are those of *Clepsydra*. This was a famous spring which must have been used far back into prehistoric times. It is said that the earlier name of the spring was Empedo, but because the well never flooded and its water could not be seen, it was given the name of Water-stealer. Early in the fifth century BC a rectangular building was constructed in front of the basin, together with an L-shaped colonnade. In Roman times, rocks fell into the basin and different arrangements had to be made so that the Athenians could reach the water once more. But before long there was another landslide, and the Athenians of late antiquity gained access to the water of Clepsydra down a deep shaft which made the original spring more of a well.

In the Christian era, Clepsydra became holy water, and a chapel of The *Holy Apostles 'at the Marbles'* was built above its overgrown ruins. Under the Turks, the well was buried by rocks and forgotten. In 1822, during the brief spell in which Athens was liberated from the Turks, the scholar Pittakis found references to the well in his books and told the Greek captains about his discovery. Odysseas Androutsos, one of the Greek leaders, built a wall around the spring and a passage from the inside so that the forces defending the castle could take as much water as they needed. According to one account, Androutsos was later thrown by his rivals the Gouras faction from the Clepsydra bastion and killed. The memories attached to Clepsydra stretch back at least 3,300 years and still flow today as freely as the water from the spring.

THE ELGIN ROOM, oils, A. Archer, 1819 (British Museum).
"What the barbarians had failed to do was done by a civilised man, by Lord Elgin, when he removed the figures of Phidias which even the bombs had not touched... How cold they must be, there in the fogs of England, those noble marbles which were accustomed to the mild air of Attica, and how they must miss the ruddy rays of the sunset as they flowed, like the red colour of life itself, through their Pentelic veins!" (Gautier).

II.2 The Sanctuary of Apollo 'in the cave'

Above the Peripatus, on the north slopes of the Acropolis at a higher level than Clepsydra, is the Cave of Apollo. Pausanias calls it "the Sanctuary of Apollo in the cave", but here the god of the sun was worshipped as Apollo Pythius, under Delphic influence, as also as *Hypoacraeus* (that is, 'beneath the long rocks' and just above the secondary Pelasgian wall).

Each year, once the nine Archons (chief magistrates) of Athens had been elected and had taken their oath on the altar of Apollo Patroeus in the Agora, they came up to the cave to swear a second oath. Among the promises they made was that they would set up a gold statue to Apollo Pythius-Patroeus in the cave if they failed to rule the city properly or were found to have embezzled public money. Of course, no such statues have ever been found in the cave, nor do we have any account of any having been put there. When the nine Archons had successfully completed their term of service, they dedicated —in the cave— a marble plaque bearing sculptured wreaths of bay and myrtle, together with their names, to commemorate their year in office. Many of these plaques were found in and around the cave.

II.3 The Cave of Zeus Astrapaeus

Next to the cave of Apollo is a second cavity, dedicated to Zeus, who was worshipped here as Olympius, Astrapaeus and Ceraunius —that is, of Olympus, of the lightning and of thunder. Literary sources tell us that the Pythiasts gathered here each spring and waited for the flash of lighning (Zeus's sign to them) which would enable them to start their journey to Delphi. The Pythiasts were the representatives of Athens at the Pythian celebrations in Delphi. On their return from the Delphic sanctuary, they brought with them unpolluted fire —'new light'— with which the sanctuaries of Athens could be purified.

II.4 The Cave of Pan

Slightly to the east of the cave of Zeus Astrapaeus is a smaller and rather attractive cave dedicated to Pan, god of the forests and of shepherds. The cult of Pan came to Athens at a late date, after the victory at Marathon in 490 BC. The story goes that Pan promised Phidippides, the messenger, on his way back from Sparta after the Spartans had refused to come to the aid of Athens against the Persians, that he would help them drive off the invaders. Sure enough, Pan appeared in person on the battlefield and spread 'panic' among the barbarians, thus enabling the vastly outnumbered Athenians to win the day. In gratitude, the Athenians honoured Pan in this cave and held a torchlit procession for him every year. Little niches were carved in the rock of the cave for offerings to the god, which included statuettes, flutes (Pan-pipes) and even delicacies to eat.

The Cave of Pan is also known to us from another source: the comedy *Lysistrata* by Aristophanes, where it is the scene of the abortive erotic encounter between Myrhine and Cinesias. In the Christian era, the temple of the goat-footed god became a chapel to St Athanasius. In the late nineteenth century, a hewn icon of a saint was discovered in the chapel, which the Turks had ruined, and given the name *Alaniaris*. Very close to the Cave of Pan are the hewn steps of a Mycenean staircase leading up to the Acropolis —probably traces of an early and 'unofficial' entrance to the Sacred Rock.

II.5 The Mycenaean spring - the Cave of Herse

By the Mycenaean carvings in the rock is an impressive cave which until recently was attributed to Aglaurus. Recent research and archaeological investigation has shown that this was probably the cave of Herse, and that Aglaurus was worshipped in the much larger cave on the east side of the Acropolis. The Cave of Herse is actually a Mycenaean spring. When the Athenians were building the walls of the

Acropolis in Mycenaean times (second half of the thirteenth century BC), they struck the spring and dug until they had uncovered the precious vein of water. The well is 18 metres deep (from the surface of the Acropolis), about half of which is accounted for by the height of the cave. Steps are hewn out of the rock, and the Athenian women of Mycenaean times would have climbed down these to fill their pots with water. There must also have been wooden steps, in the form of beams resting in the hewn recesses facing each other in the rock. The mouth of the well was up on the top of the Acropolis, next to the Erechtheum.

The Mycenaean well seems to have been used for a period of about 30 years, to judge from the potsherds found in it. It was probably filled in by a landslide, and the lower part was forgotten, but not the upper section, which was used as a secret exit from the Acropolis. The Arrephorae maidens went down these steps carrying the 'secret things' of Athena on their way to the nearby sanctuary of Aphrodite in the Gardens.

II.6 The Sanctuary of Aphrodite in the Gardens

The open-air sanctuary of Aphrodite in the Gardens is located on the ancient Peripatus, very close to the Cave of Herse. Here, the cult of Aphrodite had supplanted an earlier cult of the Mycenaean goddess with the doves, who was worshipped as a fertility deity. There is, of course, no coincidence in the Mycenaean goddess of fertility and the later cult of Aphrodite sharing a sanctuary. There was another shrine to Aphrodite (Pandemos) at the south-west Mycenaean entrance to the Acropolis. It was to this sanctuary of the goddess of love and fertility that the Arrephorae brought their 'secret things'. On the wall of the sanctuary we can see the square niches cut in the rock in which the worshippers of ancient times would have placed their offerings. Many votive inscriptions to Aphrodite and Eros were found in the area. An ancient pit was recently discovered at 9 Prytaneiou St in

Plaka, beneath a house on the site of the sanctuary of Aphrodite. Such pits were often used to bury old or broken votive offerings which could not be simply thrown away because they were sacred and this one yielded some votive offerings of the highest quality, destined for the goddess of love and fertility.

Up on the wall of the Acropolis we can see the architectural members of Archaic and pre-Classical temples burned by the Persians in 480 BC, which Cimon later built into the masonry. The members from the upper parts of temples date from the Archaic period, while the half-finished drums are from the columns of the pre-Classical Parthenon which was never completed.

III. THE EAST SIDE OF THE ACROPOLIS; THE CAVE OF AGRAULUS

During recent work on the landscaping of the ancient Peripatus, an inscription was found by chance on the site on which it had been set up in antiquity, in front of the east cave. It is a resolution of 247-245 BC honouring Timocrite, priestess of the Sanctuary of Agraulus, and it ends with the decision to inscribe the vote of thanks on a stone stele and erect it in front of the Sanctuary of Agraulus. Thus we can be certain that the east cave was the Sanctuary, and perhaps when it is exca-vated it will have some exciting surprises for us.

Agraulus, daughter of Cecrops, was the favourite princess of the Athenians, and over time she became an important deity. Here, in front of her imposing sanctu-ary, Athenian boys received their arms (shield and spear) when they reached the age of eighteen, swearing the famous oath in which they promised not to bring shame upon their sacred weapons.

IV. THE SOUTH SIDE OF THE ACROPOLIS

The view of the Sacred Rock from the south is still impressive even today. To begin with, our eye is captured by the Parthenon, the glory of architecture and sculpture; then our gaze sweeps down to dwell respectfully on the places where the Word, Poetry and the harmony of Music were honoured. In the shadow of the Acropolis, the Theatre of Dionysus and the buildings adjacent to it were the focus of Athenian intellectual life, helping to achieve the feats of the Golden Age.

IV.1 The Sanctuary and Theatre of Dionysus

At the heart of this intellectual centre was the Theatre. It is called the 'Theatre of Dionysus' because it stood next to the sanctuary of the god Dionysus Eleutherius. Dionysus was called 'Eleutherius' here because his cult was brought to Athens from Eleutherae in Boeotia, along with the wooden cult statue, by an Athenian called Pegasus in the sixth century BC. Within the sacred sanctuary, a small Archaic temple was first constructed, with two columns in front of the cella in which the cult statue was housed. In the Classical era a larger temple was built, and it contained the gold and ivory statue of Dionysus made by Alcamenes.

Today, we can see the foundations of both temples and some ruins which are believed to belong to the altar of the sanctuary. On the north side, between the Archaic temple and the skene, was a circular orchestra (dancing-ground) where the worshippers of Dionysus performed the Dithyramb (a choral lyric song describing the adventures of the god). In the course of time, the Dithyramb lost its exclusively Dionysiac character and gave birth to Tragedy.

In 333 BC, Lycurgus gave the cavea of the theatre approximately the form in which we see it today. The Peripatus was incorporated into it, and formed the division between the main part of the theatre (the cavea) and the epitheatron, or upper tier. The Theatre of Dionysus experienced its greatest moments in late March and early April each year, when it was the scene of the festival called the Great Dionysia. The Great Dionysia symbolised the rebirth of Dionysus, and the victory of spring over winter. The first day of the festival began with a solemn procession

THE THEATRE OF DIONYSUS
"From this same spot, in the happy days that Athens once enjoyed, we could have watched the fleets sailing from Piraeus; we could have heard the grief of Oedipus, of Philoctetes or of Hecuba burst forth in the theatre of Dionysus, or given ear to the speeches of Demosthenes" (Chateaubriand).

at the culmination of which the cult statue of Dionysus was brought from the temple into the centre of the theatre, and ended with sacrifices and joyful feasting. On the second and third days, Dithyrambs were performed to the accompaniment of flute music, and on the evening of the third day the Athenians revelled in the 'feast of happiness' with the victors of the Dithyramb contest. This cheerful merry-making, called the *komos*, issued in the contests for dramatists, which occupied the next three days and were the centre of the festival.

Even when the city had begun to decline, Dionysius and his devotees occupied a central place in the hearts of the Athenians. But little by little the words of the great poets gave way to the roars and screeches of Roman circuses, with fights between men and wild beasts in the sacred orchestra of the theatre, which had to be redesigned for the purpose. This degradation proceeded slowly, but ineluctably. By the fifth century AD, there was an Early Christian basilica above the east side entrance to the theatre and Dionysus had descended into Hades, never to return. Yet the annual festivities marking the Carnival time are a reminder of his presence as a herald of spring.

IV.2 The Odeum

In the enlightened time of Pericles, the Odeum, a gigantic building with a roof supported on pillars, was built next to the Theatre of Dionysus on the east. The pillars of the Odeum of Pericles were taken from the Persian ships sunk at Salamis, and the building was used for the concerts of the Athenians. The hall had room for 5,000 people, and Pausanias tells us that from the outside it looked like Xerxes' tent because the roof was pyramidal. Inside, there were many similarities with the Telesterion at Eleusis.

In Plutarch's account, Pericles personally supervised the building of the Odeum, and tabled a resolution that the musical contests of the Panathenaic Festival be held there. It is said, too, that he determined the prizes and was involved in the organisation of the various events (for the flute, the cithara, and singing). Music was deeply rooted in every aspect of ancient Greek life, and played a part as important as sculpture, poetry, the theatre and architecture. It was central to the drama, where music was a vital part of the theatrical performance and essential for its success. Unfortunately, however, only some fragments of ancient musical 'scores' have come down to us.

The Odeum of Pericles was destroyed in 86 BC when the Roman general Sulla attacked Athens. In fact, the Athenians set fire to it themselves, to prevent Sulla from using the timber in his siege campaign. Twenty five years later, it was rebuilt by King *Ariobarzanes* II of Cappadocia. Pausanias saw the rebuilt structure, about a century after its construction.

Before the beginning of the drama contests, the Odeum was the scene of the *proagon*. This was the first 'act' in the Dionysiac festivities, a kind of introduction to the programme of dramatic performances which would themselves come before the *agon*, or contest of the poets. In the crowded Odeum, the poets, actors, sponsors and chorus were presented to the audience, wearing wreaths. Each poet introduced the actors and the chorus who would be performing his play, and explained the title and plot of his work. The ceremony performed roughly the same function as a theatre poster does today.

Today, the site of the ancient Odeum contains a tiny church dedicated to St George 'of Alexandria'. It stands on the sanctuary of a much older church which was ruined in 1826, during the Greek War of Independence. In Turkish times, this was a part of the city where many Greeks lived. When the tide of war swept through Athens in August 1826, the Greeks defended the area, but on 15 August (feast day of Our Lady) the Turks set up a cannon near the church in the hope of overcoming the Greek resistance. The defenders managed to lure many of the

Turks into the church and then blew it up, killing them. That was the end of the original Church of St George 'of Alexandria'.

IV.3 The Street of the Tripods - the Choregi

We owe the name 'Street of the Tripods' to Pausanias, who tells us it was the favourite walk of the ancient Athenians, since they could stroll along it, in the shadow of the Acropolis and surrounded by superb works of art.

The Street of the Tripods was six metres wide and 800 metres long, describing a wide curve that linked the ancient Agora with the Theatre of Dionysus. It takes its name from the choregic tripods with kettles which were set in miniature temples or on columns to the right and left of the street. A long section of the Street of the Tripods coincides with the modern street bearing the same name *(odos Tripodon)* and with Lysikratous Square, both in Plaka.

The choregic tripod with its kettle was the prize awarded to the choregos —the name given to rich Athenian citizens or resident aliens whose fortune exceeded three talents and on whom the state imposed, in lieu of other taxation, the duty of paying the cost of a theatrical performance. It was the custom for the choregos - sponsor, in fact- of the winning play to build a choregic monument in the Street of the Tripods on which he set the tripod itself and its (usually gilded) kettle to commemorate his victory.

IV.4 The Monument of Thrasyllus

The closest surviving choregic monument to the Theatre of Dionyus is that of Thrasyllus, which is beneath the walls of the Acropolis, above the theatre. It is in the form of a hewn cave, and functions as a church.

In 319 BC, when Neaechmus was Archon, Thrasyllus the son of Thrasyllus of Decelia won a victory as choregos. In order to commemorate his win, he hewed a

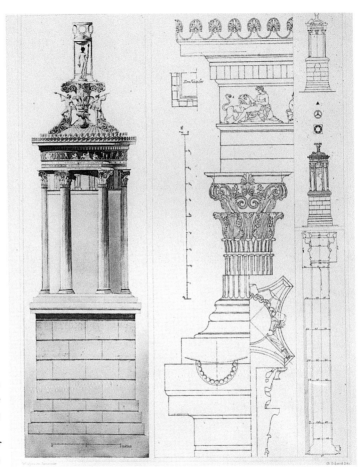

THE CHOREGIC MONUMENT OF LYSICRATES (334 BC), Collection of Eleni Leptourgos

cavity in the rock out to the dimensions of a cave and build a monumental temple-like facade across its mouth. Above it, on a plinth with three steps, he set the choregic tripod. Fifty years later, his son Thrasycles won two more victories (in the contests for the men's and children's choruses) as President of the Games, and he added two more tripods to his father's monument, one to the left and one to the right of the original. Around 400 AD, when Phaedrus renovated the Theatre, the Monument of Thrasyllus seems to have been modified. The choregic tripods were lost, and a statue of Dionysus seated was placed where the middle tripod had been. In the Christian era, the Monument of Thrasyllus was converted into a church dedicated to Our Lady 'of the Cave', and the imposing facade of antiquity was retained. Inside, naturally enough, things were changed so that the building could function as a church, with its sanctuary on the east side. Since the Athenians were fond of attaching the epithet 'gold' to Our Lady, the church became that of Our Lady 'of the Golden Cave'.

Early in the nineteenth century, the statue of Dionysus -now without its head- attracted the covetous gaze of Lord Elgin and joined the other art-works on the trip to London. And in January 1827, when Kiutaya was attacking the Acropolis, some of the Greek defenders of the castle took up position in front of the Monument of Thrasyllus; the Turks turned their cannon on the monument and the shells destroyed it completely.

IV.5 The Asclepieum

Above the Stoa of Eumenes, at the same height as the Peripatus next to the Theatre of Dionysus, are the ruins of the Sanctuary of Asclepius. The cult of Asclepius came late to Athens, arriving at the time of the Peloponnesian War and not direct from Epidaurus, where the worship of the god of medicine had its headquarters, but from the Asclepieum of Piraeus. That sanctuary had been founded a few months previously, on the east coast of the Zea promontory. The cult picture of Asclepius had been brought from Epidaurus specially for the purpose, together with a sacred snake.

The precinct contained a plain temple containing the statues of Asclepius and his daughter Hygeia. To the east of this was an altar, for sacrifices. To the north, higher on the Sacred Rock, was the Stoa of Incubation or *Katagogion*, a two-storeyed portico where the patients slept on the skins of the animals which had been slaughtered. It was said that in their sleep they dreamed of Asclepius, who advised them as to the type of treatment they should follow. At the west end of the Stoa was a square room in the centre of which was a circular shaft down which the remains of the sacrifices were disposed of— they, too, were sacred. Perhaps there may have been sacred snakes, as there certainly were at Epidaurus; their venom was used in making the medicines dispensed by the sanctuary.

Deep in the heart of the Acropolis rock was another spring, whose clear waters were used to clean and purify the patients of the Asclepieum. Among the other buildings on the site were a monumental gateway, a Roman stoa and a hostel.

In antiquity, there were some 320 sanctuaries of Asclepius around the known world. Each was a combination of temple, hospital and medical school. Patients who arrived in search of treatment described their symptoms to the priests, who drew up a plan of therapy. When the first stage of this had been completed, the patient formally entered the precinct of Asclepius, taking with him votive offerings and a baby animal -usually a kid- for sacrifice. After purification and the appropriate rituals, the animal was sacrificed and the patient then took its skin and headed for the Stoa of Incubation.

The priests of the sanctuary were trained doctors and, in order to practise, they had to have studied for six years, just as is the case today. They were also obliged to spend the rest of their lives in the Asclepieum, which meant that they acquired great experience in medical matters. They administered medicines, most of them made from medicinal herbs, of which the ancient author Dioscurides had identified and classified 630 species. We know for certain that the priests often performed surgical operations: instruments identical in shape and function to those still used today have been found in Asclepieums all over Greece. The root of the mandragora seems to have been one of the anaesthetics used.

In the Christian era (fifth century AD) Asclepius was succeeded by the physician-saints Cosmas and Damian. At this time, a three-aisled basilica dedicated to them was built on top of the sanctuary and temple of the pagan god. The sacred spring may have been used for baptism at this time. Later, when the Christian basilica disappeared in the turmoil of the long centuries of Athenian history, the cave with the spring became a church to Our Lady 'the Life-Receiving Fount'. Today, among the scattered stones which make it difficult even to guess at which of the ancient buildings of the Asclepieum was which, the cave of Our Lady is still there as a reminder of the unbroken continuity of religious worship in Athens.

IV.6 The Stoa of Eumenes

On the south side of the Acropolis, between the Herodes Atticus Theatre and the Theatre of Dionysus, the walls and arches of the Stoa of Eumenes can still be seen. This was an addition to the Theatre of Dionysus, used for the selling of refreshments and as a promenade during the breaks in the theatrical performances. It also served as a shelter when the weather was bad - in other words, it was something like the foyer of a modern theatre.

The Stoa was built early in the second century BC by Eumenes II, King of Pergamum. It was two-storeyed, and had a length of 163 metres. It stood on the retaining wall of the Peripatus and had, on the ground floor, a Doric colonnade on the outside and an Ionic colonnade within. On the upper floor, there were double

Ionic half-columns on the outside and fine columns of the Pergamum order on the inside. When the Herod Atticus Theatre was built next to the Stoa 3,5 centuries later, the new structure blended so well with the older one that it came to be believed that the Stoa of Eumenes was built for it and not the Theatre of Dionysus.

The Stoa continued in use until the third century AD, when it was demolished so that its materials could be used in the Valerian wall of Athens. Some of its architectural members have been identified in a house in Veikou St. Today, the ruined Stoa of Eumenes has little of its ancient grandeur, but, if we want to see what it must have looked like, we can visit the Stoa of Attalus in the ancient Agora. It was built a few years later by Eumenes' brother, Attalus II of Pergamum, and has been reconstructed as it was in antiquity to give a taste of Athenian splendour.

IV.7 The Choregic Monument of Nicias and the Tomb of Talus

Between the Stoa of Eumenes and the Theatre of Dionysus are the foundations of the small Choregic Monument of Nicias, erected in 319 BC to commemorate Nicias' victory as a choregos. The monument was in the form of a prostyle Doric temple, whose entrance had to be on the west side because the east was occupied by the wall retaining the cavea of the Theatre. It was demolished in the late antiquity and its materials used in building the Beulé Gate on the Acropolis. There is thus very little to differentiate the ruins of this monument from all the others in the area.

According to Pausanias (second century AD), the Tomb of *Talus* or *Calus* was between the Asclepieum and the Theatre. Calus was the son of Perdica and the nephew of Daedalus, and he was credited with having invented the saw, the compasses and the potter's wheel. Calus' uncle Daedalus, afraid that the youth would outdo him in ingenuity, threw him off the Acropolis, whereupon Perdica committed suicide and Daedalus himself was exiled to Crete. According to one version of the story, Daedalus repented of his crime and built a kind of mythological robot in memory of his nephew Talus.

IV.8 The Archaic Spring

On the west side of the Asclepieum, above the Stoa of Eumenes, is an Archaic fountain which can be admired even today. It may have been dedicated to Alcippe, daughter of Aglaurus and Ares and the favourite nymph of the Athenians.

According to the myths, it was here that Ares killed Halirrhotius, son of Poseidon, for having had the temerity to defile Alcippe. Poseidon demanded that Ares be punished, but the gods, meeting in assembly on the Areopagus, declared the god of war innocent.

The Archaic masonry of the fountain has survived in excellent condition, as has an Archaic inscription marking the boundary between the spring, the Asclepieum and the Peripatus. In the Byzantine period, two cisterns were built here to provide water for the troops defending the castle.

The nymph Alcippe was probably also worshipped at a sanctuary found to the south of the Herodes Atticus Theatre, beneath the houses in Dionysiou Areopagitou St. The site yielded a large quantity of votive offerings, and in particular loutrophoroi (ewers), the vases connected with weddings. The offerings may have been from the maidens of Athens, who wished to invoke the assistance of the nymph in obtaining a happy marriage.

Next to the fountain, Pausanias describes a temple dedicated to Themis, goddess of justice, and an imposing monument to Hippolytus in front of it.

IV.9 The Odeum of Herodes Atticus

Today, the most impressive monument on the south side of the Acropolis is the Odeum (now usually called the 'Theatre') of Herodes Atticus. Philostratus tells us

THE ODEUM OF HERODES ATTICUS.

that in around 160 AD Regilla, the wife of Herodes, died, and he built this superb structure in memory of her. Even today, it is possible to tell from the construction of the skene and the facade, with its fragmentary mosaics, ornamental niches and other costly features, that this was a building on which no expense was spared. The facade was three-storeyed, with large apertures leading up to arches. Today, the marble statues and the columns which once decorated the facade have vanished, and the niches are the home only to pigeons.

It seems that when the Theatre was built it did not have an entrance through the facade as it does today. Earlier buildings blocked the access on this side, and so the theatre was entered from the side, through the Stoa of Eumenes. Inside, the *proskenion* (stage wall) had ornamental niches in which stood fine marble columns. The tiers in the cavea -that is, the seating for the audience- was faced with marble, too. To gain some idea of what the theatre looked like in antiquity, we can easily imagine the seating with its marble facing (the capacity of 5,000 is the same as it was then), but it is more difficult to recreate in the mind the magnificent roof, constructed entirely in costly cedar. The roof covered the entire cavea without supports, not an unusual achievement for the advanced technology of the day.

The barbaric raid of the Heruli in 267 BC proved fatal for the incomparable theatre: they set fire to it, and the cedar roof collapsed. Little by little, the site was abandoned and the theatre filled up with earth. Under the Turks, the theatre was incorporated into the fortifications of the Acropolis; it was a bastion in the Serpentzes wall (the name means 'strong' or 'formidable'), and was one of the most impregnable parts of the entire defensive system.

There can be no doubt that the south side of the Sacred Rock, with all its monuments, functioned as the intellectual and educational centre of Greece -and indeed of the entire ancient world. Its uniqueness is accentuated still further by the fact that this area, with its grouping of artistic buildings and events in integrated sections, served as a model of urban planning first for the whole of Greece and then for the entire world.

IV.10 The Areopagus

To the north west, the Sacred Rock of the Acropolis has a lower companion in the hill of Areopagus. There were numerous stories about the origin of its name, which are summarised by Pausanias in his description of Attica (I, 28, 5). From the etymological point of view, *pagus* means 'rock', and so we have a rock dedicated either to Ares or to the Arae, another name for the Furies, goddesses of vengeance. The name of the rock was also applied to the outdoor Court of antiquity, whose life-members were all Archons who had successfully completed their term of service. It had great power in the period when Athens was ruled by an oligarchic system, but in 456 BC the democrat Ephialtes persuaded the Ecclesia of the Deme to pass resolutions stripping the Areopagus of many of its responsibilities. After that time, it dealt exclusively with religious issues.

The hill changed in appearance in 1651, when a major earthquake split it in two and demolished the Church of St Dionysius and the sanctuaries of the Furies, of Boreas and of the Amazons, which stood on its lower slopes. On the top were the Stone of Injury, on which the accused stood, and the Stone of Ruthlessness, which was the position of the 'prosecutor'. It is believed that this is the place where, in 54 AD, St Paul, Apostle to the Gentiles, preached on the Unknown God, making Dionysius the Areopagite his first Athenian convert to Christianity.

IV. 11 The Hill of the Muses - Philopappus

On the top of the hill are the foundations of a fortified precinct built in 294 BC by *Demetrius Poliorcetes*, King of Macedonia, as a barracks for his garrison. In 115 BC, the Athenians of late antiquity erected a funerary monument to Philopappus, a descendant of the Seleucid kings.

In 1954-57, the architect and thinker Dimitris Pikionis landscaped the area of the hills of the Acropolis, the Areopagus and the Nymphs and Muses, and we walk along his paths there today.

IV.12 The Hill of the Nymphs - the Pnyx

The Pnyx is close to, and facing, the Acropolis, as befits its important role. After the late sixth century BC, the Pnyx was the venue of the Ecclesia of the Deme - that is, the assembly of Athenian citizens. A fifth-century boundary marker shows that the function of the site was determined by that time, and the name *'pnyx'* comes from the adjective meaning 'dense', showing how compact the site was. Originally, the meeting-place was differently aligned, and the members of the assembly looked towards the Acropolis. But in 404-403 BC it was observed that people's eyes strayed towards the monuments there and they tended to lose their concentration, so the positions of speaker and audience were reversed. At this time the semicircle of seating was extended, a retaining wall was built, and staircases were installed at the sides. Under Lycurgus (330-326 BC), the site came to look more or less as it does today, and the *bema* (rostrum) was hewn out of the natural rock. Next to it are carved niches for votive offerings to Zeus Hypsistus. It is believed that above the bema was the altar to Zeus Agoraeus, which was later taken to the Agora. To the SW, the site of Meton's sundial has been identified. In the late fourth century BC, the meetings of the Ecclesia were moved to the Theatre of Dionysus. Between the Hill of the Nymphs and the nearby Hill of the Muses was the *diateichisma*, one of the sections in the city's defensive wall.

V. THE ANCIENT AGORA

Below the immortal monuments of the Acropolis, the more modest ruins of the Agora make much less of an impression on the visitor. Fortunately, the Temple of Hephaestus (popularly known as the Theseum) and the Stoa of Attalus, at either side of the Agora, are still there to underscore the importance of what was the centre of Athenian public life.

The word Agora comes from the verb *agoreuo*, which means to speak in public.

This etymology is directly connected with the varied role of the Agora in the everyday life of the ancient Athenians: it was the seat of government and of the judicial system, and it was also the place where trade and business were conducted. In pre-Classical times, the Agora was also the meeting-place of the Ecclesia of the Deme, and the venue for theatrical performances and athletic contests.

Throughout Athenian history and down to late antiquity -more specifically, to 267 AD when it was totally destroyed by the Heruli- the Agora was also the place where the Athenians led their social and intellectual lives. In a nutshell, it was the heart of the city.

V.1 The Temple of Hephaestus (Theseum)

On the low hill of Colonus Agoraeus, the highest point in the Agora, stands the Temple of Hephaestus, the best-preserved temple of Classical antiquity. Here the god of fire and metal was jointly worshipped with Athena, protector of the city, as the patrons of the crafts and professions -and more specifically of the metalworkers and potters. In our own day, just as in antiquity, the shops of metalworkers stand almost next to the temple.

The Temple of Hephaestus was the first project in the ambitious programme of building proposed by Pericles. Work on it began before the Parthenon was started, which explains why its exterior is obviously older than the temple on the Acropolis, but construction was suspended while Athena's temple was erected and resumed after it was finished. It was planned by the important, but nameless to us, architect who designed and built at least three more famous temples: of Poseidon at Sunium, of Ares at Acharnae (subsequently moved to the Agora and now in a ruinous state), and of Nemesis at Ramnous. All four are imposing peripteral structures with the same architectural details, layout and refinements as found on the Parthenon.

The temple was divided into a pronaos, a cella and an *opisthodomos*. The cella had an interior double colonnade which imitated that of the Parthenon. In it were the cult statues of Hephaestus and Athena Erganes, made by the sculptor Alcamenes. The *metopes*, the interior frieze (influenced by that of the Parthenon) and the pediments bore scenes from the feats of the two great heroes, Theseus and Heracles. It was the presence of Theseus that caused the confusion and the misidentification of the monument.

In the Christian period, the temple was converted into a church of St George - which in Turkish times acquired the nickname *Akamatis*, meaning 'the lazy one', because services were only permitted there once a year, on the saint's day. Until the archaeological excavations began the whole area was a kind of 'lovers' lane'. When foreign visitors started to come to Athens, the church was used as a burial ground for those who happened to die in the city. The temple still contains the tombstones, with Latin inscriptions, of the foreigners whose fate it was to leave their bones in Greek soil. There are graffiti, too, carved by foreign admirers of Greece in the marbles of the temple: Spon, Poqueville, Choiseul-Gouffier, Chateaubriand and other less well-known figures scratched their names indelibly on the white marble. The 'stone chronicle' of Turkish-occupied Athens is there, too: the Athenians -some of them famous figures, most anonymous, used the walls and columns of the Theseum to record their experiences, their sufferings and their griefs.

The last time 'St George' was used as a church was for the *Te Deum* to mark the arrival of King Othon in Athens, on 1 December 1834. Shortly afterwards, the building became a museum. In 1835, the Holy Synod of the Church of Greece resolved "to remove from the building the Holy Altar and any other object located therein that might designate it as a church". The job of converting the monument was taken on by the Bavarian architect Schaubert, associate of Stamatis Kleanthes. The vaulted roof of the Byzantine church was covered with slabs of Maltese

THE TEMPLE OF HEPHAESTUS in the ancient Agora.

limestone, the sanctuary was demolished, and the temple regained its original pagan appearance.

Until Liberation in 1830, the main gateway to Athens from Piraeus -the Aslan Kapuyi or Dragon Gate- was near the temple. Piraeus at this time was called Porto Leone or Porto Draco because of the marble lion which had stood at the entrance to the harbour since ancient times. It ultimately fell victim to Morosini's mania for collecting statues of lions, and now adorns the Arsenal in the Serene Republic of Venice. Here, too, was the fifth gate in the low eighteenth century wall built by Hasekis, what Skouzes called in his Memoirs the "Mandravili gate to the north west". The name came from a lady practical doctor who was a member of the Mandravilis family, of Albanian descent, who lived nearby.

Today, the silence of the museum reigns in the temple of Hephaestus. The glories of the past have departed, and the Church of St George no longer functions. The Aslan Kapuyi and the Mandravili gate have been demolished, and the lady doctor is a legend. The lion, too, has gone from Piraeus and can be seen in Venice. Lovers no longer haunt the 32 columns, the drums and clarinets have fallen silent, and the grassy fields have disappeared beneath the concrete. But the marble columns of the god of fire stand firmly in place, and above them the carved ships voyage on into eternity.

V.2 The administrative centre
Beneath the Temple of Hephaestus and the hill of Colonus Agoraeus was the centre of Athenian administration, consisting of the Prytaneum, the Bouleuterion and the Metroön, the small temple of Zeus Phratrius and Athena Phratria and of Apollon Patroeus, the Stoa of Zeus Eleutherius and the Stoa Basileius.

V.2.a The Bouleuterion
In the Archaic period, the *Boule* ('council') of the Athenians probably met in the open air, on approximately the same site. When democracy became established in Athens, the Old Bouleuterion (early fifth century BC) was built beneath the site later occupied by the Metroön. This was a spacious hall with interior columns. On three sides around the area of the rostrum for the speakers and the altar was seating arranged in tiers. In front, there was a low railing, behind which, in the antechamber, ordinary citizens could stand and watch the proceedings, just as happens in a modern parliament. The New Bouleuterion was erected on approximately the same site late in the fifth century BC. Under the Thirty Tyrants, the Boule was convened as a court before which the democratic Athenians were arraigned, and appalling acts of violence were committed under the threat of the Tyrants' weapons. In the years when the power of Athens was at its height, the Boule had five hundred members, which is why it is normally called the Council

of 500. Each of the ten 'tribes' of Athens chose 50 council members by drawing lots, and their term of service lasted a year. In ancient Athens, only the generals and the leading citizens entrusted with the management of the public funds were elected, all the other officials being chosen by lot, and all posts were salaried. After the lots had been drawn, the prospective council members were examined: that is, the Council investigated their doings down to that point in time, their personalities and their private lives.

V.2.b The Tholos

Next to the Bouleuterion on the south side was another important building, the Tholos (also known as the *Skias* or *Prytaneum*). This was a simple round structure, and it was the seat of the Athenian government. Originally erected under Cimon, in the pre-Classical period, it kept its plain circular layout throughout the subsequent building phases.The Tholos was the headquarters of the Council's 50 Prytaneis, or Presidents. The Prytaneis dined in the Tholos each day, in a routine closely bound up with religious ritual. Because of this common meal -which was a continuation of a religious rite that began with a sacrifice, and was intended to ensure the favour of the gods- there was a kitchen next to the Tholos. The Prytaneis also sacrificed before meetings of the Ecclesia, to *Apollo Prostaterius* (the Protector) and Artemis Phosphorus. Artemis Phosphorus (a capacity linked to Artemis Boulaea, of the Boule) was so called because her cult in the Tholos was shared with the Phosphores, minor chthonic deities who protected the public life of the city. The sanctity of the Tholos was such that it was the place where the official weights and measures were kept.

The Tholos was not only the seat of the Prytaneis and the focus of the Athenian administration, but also a sacred place where the deities who protected public life were worshipped. The building was the heart of ancient Athens, that ideal state with its flawless democratic system of government.

THE AGORA CIRCA THE END OF THE 2ND CENTURY A.D.

21. Altar of the Twelve Gods
29. Triangular shrine
30. Theseum
31. Enneakrounos
35. Panathenaic Way
36. Temple of Hephaestus
37. Stoa of Zeus Eleutherius
38. New Bouleuterium
39. Tholos
40. Strategeium
41. South-west Fountain House
45. Stoa Poikile
46. Stoa of the Herms
47. Temple of Zeus Phratrius and Athena Phratria
48. Temple of Apollo Patroös
49. Eponymous Heroes
50. Bouleuterium propylon
51. Middle Stoa
52. East Building
54. Temple of Aphrodite
55. East Building
56. Metroön
57. South Stoa II
58. Stoa of Attalus
59. Bema
60. Hippomachia Gate
61. Stoa of the Roman period
62. Kerameikos boundary stone
63. North-east Stoa
64. Round Fountain House
65. Odeum of Agrippa
66. Altar of Zeus Agoraeus
67. Temple and altar of Ares
71. South-east Temple
72. Nymphaeum
73. Latrines
74. Library of Pantaenus
75. South-east Stoa.

(I. Travlos)

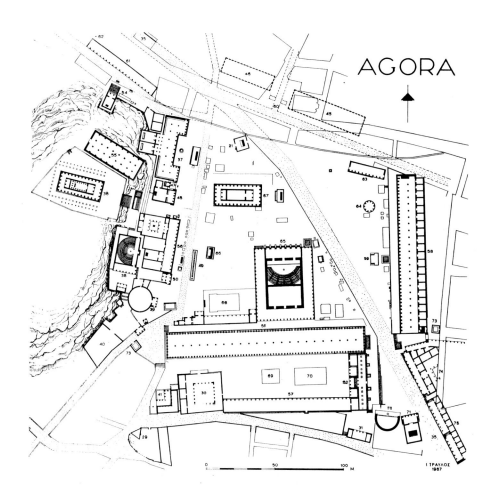

AGORA

I. ΤΡΑΥΛΟΣ
1967

V.2.c The Metroön

Among the ruins of the Old Bouleuterium and of the Archaic Metroön, which the Persians destroyed, we can pick out the remains of the Hellenistic Metroön. The building took its name from its dedication to the Mother *(Meter)* of the gods. In earlier times, there was a cult of the earth-goddess *Gaea* here, who later became identified with her daughter Rhea (or Cybele). This led to a further conflation with the goddess Demeter, whose cult was also associated with the earth, and also with the Great Mother, whose cult was imported from Phrygia in the east.

The building consisted of four rooms. The first and third were use for the keeping of the public records. The second was arranged as a temple in which the Mother of the Gods was worshipped —in other words, this was the Metroön proper. The fourth, on the north side, was larger than the others and was in the form of a residence with an atrium (interior courtyard), and may have been the state apartments in which official visitors were accommodated. In the sanctuary of the temple was a striking statue of the goddess, which showed her seated with a cymbal; next to her were proud lions, drawing her chariot into eternity.

In the Metroön, all the originals of all the public resolutions were deposited, inscribed on papyrus, leather or wooden plaques. The Athenian state employed a special clerk whose job it was to arrange these documents and keep them in good order. When necessary, he produced official copies of the documents for the public officials and the courts, and he was also the source of copies of resolutions which were to be engraved on columns and set up in public places. The building was also a repository for certificates of birth and marriage, thus explaining why its name is still (in Modern Greek) the ordinary word for an official register. The fact that the temple of the Mother of the Gods was also the public archives stemmed from the belief that the Great Goddess protected such things, and there was thus a connection between her cult and the political life of Athens from a very early date. Outside the Metroön, archaeologists found a large storage jar similar to that in which the Stoic philosopher Diogenes is said to have lived. Time and waves of invaders may have swept all before them, but apart from the stone foundations of the building its memory still lives on in Modern Greek terminology -and in the reconstruction by our imaginations of a picture of Diogenes engaged in his search for the sun, for light and for a truly just man.

V.2.d The Temple of Apollo Patroös

Next to this imposing structure was a small temple dedicated to Apollo Patroös. This was a simple tetrastyle structure of the fourth century BC, built on the foundations of an Archaic temple which the Persians had destroyed. Inside the temple was a magnificent statue of Apollo Patroös by the renowned sculptor Euphranor. In the entrance -*pronaos*- to the temple, Pausanias admired two statues of Phoebus Apollo by Calames and Leochares, but these have long since vanished.

The sun-god was worshipped here as Patroös (pater, father) because it was believed that he was the 'father' of the Ionians, and thus of the Athenians. In the myths, Apollo was the father of Ion, from whom the Ionian race traced its descent.

There was a connection between the cult of Apollo in this temple and that of Apollo Hypoacraeus, who was worshipped on the north slopes of the Acropolis. It was here that the Archons of the city took their first oath each year, and Apollo was generally recognised as the patron of the organisation of the city-state. He was also connected with the Athenian 'brotherhoods' (see below).

V.2.e The Temple of Zeus Phratrius and Athena Phratria

Directly to the north of the temple of Apollo Patroös was a small, simple Classical temple to a related cult, that of the great deities of Zeus Phratrius and Athena Phratria. These epithets are from a root cognate with the Latin *frater*, meaning 'brother', and they were attached here to the Olympian deities Zeus and Athena because they were worshipped as the patrons of the Athenian brotherhoods ('phratriai'). There were quite a number of these brotherhoods in Athens, and they were groups of blood-related families which kept up close bonds. Every Athenian citizen had to belong to one of the brotherhoods.

In the little temple were the cult statues of Zeus and Athena. Next to the two temples (of Apollo Patroös and of Zeus Phratrius and Athena Phratria) was an altar at which the members of each Athenian brotherhood offered up joint sacrifices in honour of all three gods. The joint sacrifices took place on the third day of the civil festival known as the *Apaturia*, during which the children born during the previous year were enrolled in the brotherhoods. It also involved the presentation to the brotherhoods of the young men and women who had reached maturity. In the case of the boys, the ceremony was called the Koureia, while for the girls its name was Meion -the 'minor ceremony'. This is a reflection of the low status of women in ancient Athens -one of the few disadvantages of what was otherwise an incomparably democratic system.

V.2.f The Stoa of Zeus Eleutherius

In the adminstrative centre of the city stood another important public building, the Stoa of Zeus Eleutherius. This colonnade, built in the golden years of Pericles, was built on the foundations of an Archaic temple to the father of the gods, and Zeus was worshipped as Eleutherius because of his role in saving the Greeks from the Persians. And it was said, too, that "no one is truly free except Zeus".

In the centre of the colonnade was an imposing statue of Zeus Eleutherius. Next to this, in the late Roman period, a statue was set up to a Roman personality who had the good fortune to receive the divine epithet of Eleutherius himself: this was the Emperor Hadrian, for whose generous gifts to their city the Athenians had every reason to be grateful. Today, the statue of Hadrian -mutilated and headless-lies a few metres from the ruins of the colonnade. In the Roman era, two extra rooms like small temples were added behind the west wall of the Stoa of Zeus Eleutherius. It has been suggested that these were used for the worship, together with Zeus Eleutherius, of the two Liberators of Roman times -that is, the Emperors Augustus and Hadrian.

Pausanias mentions the superb paintings with which the walls of the Stoa were decorated. The twelve gods, Theseus depicted with personifications of Democracy and the Deme, and scenes from the Battle of Mantinea lent particular magnificence to this Stoa, which was both a sacred and a public building. The paintings were the work of Euphranor of Isthmia, a famous painter, sculptor and theoretician of art of the fourth century BC. Some relics of the ancient glory of Athens were on display in the Stoa of Zeus Eleutherius, including the shields of brave warriors who had fallen in the service of their country, and various democratic resolutions.

According to the Dialogues of Plato, the benches in the Stoa were the favourite meeting-place of the philosophers of Athens, and Xenophon, in his *Oeconomicus*, tells us that Socrates debated with Ischomachus in the sacred Colonnade. This was another of the haunts of Diogenes, who used to say how grateful he was to the Athenians for having built a colonnade in honour of Zeus so that he, too, could have a place to shelter.

V.2.g The Stoa Basileius

At the north-west corner of the ancient Agora, in between the railway lines, the traces of another fine building -the Stoa Basileius- can today only just be discerned. The colonnade took its epithet (meaning 'royal'), from the fact that this was the seat of the Archon-King, one of the nine officials elected by the city each year to deal with religious and procedural matters.

The Stoa Basileius was one of the most famous public buildings of the city, with a history that stretches back to the Archaic period. It was rebuilt after the Persian invasion, and shortly afterwards small wings were added to the right and left of the facade and gave the building still greater grandeur.

Aristotle tells us that when the Athenians agreed to accept the laws of Solon and cease using the strict code of Draco, they inscribed the new statutes on wooden pillars which they set up in the Stoa Basileius, swearing that they would obey them. Further inscriptions were added later, giving all the subsequent legislation of Athens. In the centre was an imposing statue of Themis, goddess of justice, in front of which was the 'oath stone' -a simple altar at which the Archons took their oath of allegiance. The oath bound them to respect the laws and warned that should they prove to be oath-breakers their entire families would be exterminated.

In the Stoa Basileius, the Archon-King conducted the preliminary investigations into cases of sacrilege and murder -which is why the initial stages in the trial of Socrates took place on this spot. The Archon-King was also engaged in the organisation of the traditional festivals, contests and secret rituals of the Athenians. At the spring festival of the *Anthesteria*, he played the role of Dionysus, and on the second day of the feast his wife was married to Dionysus in a symbolic wedding. On this day, too, there was a wine-drinking contest, and the whole Agora was even busier than usual.

The Athenian devotees of Dionysus, in a state of euphoria caused by the wine, rode on carts round and in front of the Stoa Basileius. It was the custom for the revellers to shout insults at each other -and the phrase "to hear it from the carts" is still used in Modern Greek to mean getting a stiff ticking off, in a phrase that goes straight back to the cult of Dionysus in ancient Athens.

FAUVEL'S HOUSE, lithograph, Louis Dupré, Paris 1825.

V.3 The Monument of the Eponymous Heroes

Hippothoön, Antiochus, Ajax, Leos, Erechtheus, Aegeus, Oeneus, Acamas, Cecrops, Pandion -those are the names of the legendary heroes who became patrons of the ten eponymous (i.e., bearing their names) 'tribes' into which the population of Attica was divided by Cleisthenes. In the Classical period, the Athenians set up a monument to honour the heroes in the Agora, the heart of their city. Because of its importance, the monument was erected at the very centre of the Agora, in front of the Prytaneum and the Bouleuterium from which the city was administered. It consisted of a large, elongated plinth on which stood bronze statues of the city's eponymous heroes.

In the Hellenistic period, the Athenians wished to honour Antigonus, King of Macedonia, and his son Demetrius Poliorcetes, and they did so by founding two new 'tribes' which bore their names.Their statues thus had to be added to the monument of the eponymous heroes, and this was done by extending the plinth to the north and south. Later, these 'tribes' were abolished once more, and the statues removed -only to be replaced by a new set of eponymous heroes (Attalus, Ptolemy and Hadrian) for whom 'tribes' had been formed. The ends of the plinth of the monument were ornamented with large bronze tripods.

The importance of this monument is that it functioned as an information centre for the Athenians -rather like an ancient Athenian newspaper. On the base of the plinth whitewashed wooden boards were hung, and public announcements and pieces of news were written on these. The upper part of the plinth had a protruding ledge which helped to keep these boards dry when it was raining. Citizens could lean over the chest-high stone wall in front of the monument and read the various announcements at their leisure. Under the statue of its eponymous hero, each 'tribe' hung up a notice with the names of the adolescents who were liable for military service - and of the Athenians who were to be conscripted in time of war.

The orator Demosthenes tells us that members of the council (and ordinary Athenian citizens) could use notices hung on the monument to announce new laws that they wished to propose, doing so a few days before the meeting of the Ecclesia of the Deme so as to ensure that the citizens had time to think about what they would be voting on. We know from literary sources that the *Thesmothetes*, the officials responsible for monitoring the laws passed, hung notices on the monument commenting on these proposed laws. Another purpose of the notices was to inform the citizens about special distinctions awarded to Athenians who had performed outstanding services to the city or for Democracy.

V.4 The Altar of the Twelve Gods

Part of the precinct of the Sanctuary of the Twelve Gods can just be distinguished among the vegetation by the wall of the railway line. Pausanias calls this the Altar of Mercy, dedicated to the god of generosity. Undeniable testimony to the site of the modest sanctuary is provided by the inscription that can be seen in the overgrown stones: "Leander, son of Glaucon, dedicated this statue" (which has disappeared) "to the Twelve Gods".

Thucydides tells us that Pisistratus, son of Hippias -bearer of his grandfather's famous name- founded a sanctuary of the Twelve Gods of Olympus in the Agora. The sanctuary was a square fenced area with an altar in the middle. It was destroyed by Xerxes' Persians and rebuilt by the Athenians towards the end of the Golden Age.

Since the altar of the twelve gods was in a central position in the Agora, it was used as the point from which all distances were measured, the purpose served by Syntagma Square in modern Athens. The sanctuary was also the safest place of refuge for fugitives -and it must have kept this role into Roman times, which is why Pausanias terms it the 'altar of mercy'. Philostratus tells us that Mercy ('Eleos') was worshipped by the Athenians as a thirteenth god. No blood sacrifices or even bloodless offerings were made to this newcomer in the Pantheon: human tears were his only ex-votos.

The Athenians set up altars to other personifications of qualities, including *Aido* ('shame'), *Horme* ('impulse') and *Pheme* ('glory'). Pausanias believed that the

Athenians were more fortunate than other mortals because "it is clear that those whose piety is rather better-developed than others also tend to be happier".

V.5 The first theatre - the Lenaeum

The first theatre in Athens was in the centre of the Agora. When, in the Archaic period, the area of the Agora was turned over to public use, a circular orchestra was laid out for the dancing involved in festivals for the entire city. It must have looked rather like the threshing-floors often to be seen today near Greek villages. When the cult of Dionysus was introduced, the altar to the god of wine and vegetation was set up in the centre of the orchestra. The leading 'actor' would mount the steps of the altar, while the dance went on around him. The spectators would tend to gather in a circle round the dance, to see what was going on. This ensured that there was very close contact between the actors and the audience, an essential factor in the cult of Dionysus, which demanded the complete involvement of all participants. The next step was for wooden benches to be constructed in amphitheatrical form, and for the back rows to be raised so the audience could see. The ancient sources tell us that the performances were so well-attended that a neighbouring beech tree often served as a viewpoint for those unable to find seats.

Many archaeologists have identified the theatre in the Agora with the *Lenaeum*, where a feast was held in honour of Dionysus Lenaeus -the epithet comes from a word meaning the vats where the grapes were trampled to make wine. In the theatre, it is believed, the *Lenae* or *Bacchae*, the female devotees of the god, performed their dance in honour of the god, and the theatrical contests of the Lenaea festival were held. In the Classical period, this theatre was used mainly for performances of comedy, such as Aristophanes' *Frogs*. Later, all the theatrical performances were moved to the theatre of Dionysus Eleutherius, and in Roman times the site of the historic theatre was swallowed up by the bulk of the Odeum of Agrippa.

V.6 The Temple of Ares

Between the ruins of the Altar of the Twelve Gods and those of the Odeum, a pile of broken pieces of marble serves to mark out the boundaries and dimensions of what was once the elegant Temple of Ares. The god of war was worshipped from very early times in Athens, and his cult was associated with the victory of Theseus over the Amazons. Over the many centuries of its history, the Temple of Ares suffered various vicissitudes, as evidenced by the poor state in which we see it today.

The temple was built by the important —but, to us, nameless— architect of the Golden Age who also designed the similar temples of Hephaestus (in the Agora), of Poseidon (at Sunium) and of Nemesis (at Rhamnous). The building originally stood at Acharnae (now Menidi) on the foothills of Mt Parnes. In the Roman period, it was dismantled stone by stone and moved, with its foundation, to the Agora. The temple was moved on the orders of the Emperor Augustus, and in it the god of war was worshipped together with Gaius Caesar, Augustus' deified son. Pausanias tells us that in the temple were two superb statues of Ares and Aphrodite, the work of Alcamanes. The famous Venus of Milos, which now adorns the Louvre in Paris, is said to have been a copy of the statue of Aphrodite witch was in the Temple of Ares.

V.7 The statues of the Tyrannocides

Next to the Temple of Ares the statues of the tyrannocides Harmodius and Aristogeiton, who assassinated the tyrant Hipparchus and contributed to liberating Athens from the Pisistratid dictatorship, stood proudly for many years.

After Hipparchus' brother Hippias had also been driven from the city, the Athenians set up the statues of the two youths -created by the sculptor Antenor- in a prominent position. But some years later, when Xerxes and his Persians invaded

Athens, they carried off the Archaic group of sculpture along with a great quantity of other booty and took it back to Persia. As soon as the Persians had gone, the Athenians made the creation and re-erection of the statues of the tyrannocides - symbols of liberty and democracy- among their first tasks. The statues were commissioned from the sculptors Critias and Nesiotes, and were set up on the sites of their predecessors. The originals spent more than one hundred and fifty years in Persia before Alexander the Great -or possibly one of his successors- fetched them back to Athens. And so it came about that the Tyrannocides of Antenor, those Archaic symbols of democracy, were respectfully given their rightful places next to the later group by Critias and Nesiotes.

The Athenians worshipped Harmodius and Aristogeiton, and the area around their statues was seen as sacred and functioned as a sanctuary. After sacrificing to Artemis Agrotera, the Polemarch (commander-in-chief) for the year would make offerings to the Tyrannocides. The Athenians never forgot the acts of violence which the tyrants had committed against democratic citizens.

V.8 The Stoa of Attalus

The eastern edge of the Agora is bounded by the magnificent Stoa of Attalus. This is the only ancient building in Athens which has been completely restored and rebuilt on its original foundations. The Stoa was the second monumental building with which the noble family of the Attalids from Pergamum endowed Athens, the first being the Stoa of Eumenes which King Eumenes II built on the south slopes of the Acropolis in the early second century BC. Some years later, his brother, Attalus II, erected the Stoa in the Agora as a further jewel in the city's crown. In the Hellenistic period, it was the custom for leading families throughout the Mediterranean to send their younger members to study in Athens, and Attalus II had been among those who had the city of Pallas Athena to thank for their intellectual deve-

THE STOA OF ATTALUS at the ancient Agora.

lopment. When he became king of Pergamum, he wished to honour his *altra mater* by dedicating to it this superb Stoa. The double colonnades of the upper and lower floors are a parade of almost all the ancient orders of architecture, arranged with great good taste and imagination. The alternating styles, the wealth of the materials and the interplay of light and shadow combine to produce a harmonious whole of outstanding beauty. The 43 rooms on the two floors of the Stoa of Attalus were used as shops which the Athenian state rented out to private merchants. The position of the building, on the Panathenaic Way with the best view in the whole Agora, made it an ideal place to promenade or from which to watch the processions. The staircases to the upper storey were originally on the outer side of the building, but that on the south side was moved inside around 100 AD. Today, the Stoa of Attalus can give us some taste of the unrivalled beauty of Athens in ancient times.

V.9 The Odeum of Agrippa

A few years before the birth of Christ, Agrippa, an associate and son-in-law of Augustus, added to the beauty of Athens by building a superb structure -the Odeum- almost in the centre of the Agora. The Odeum of Agrippa had seating for a thousand people and its roof was not supported by interior columns. It combined one of the boldest architectural designs of antiquity with all the elegance of the Corinthian order.

In the mid-second century BC, however, the roof collapsed and the building was seriously damaged. It seems to have been repaired fairly quickly, but henceforth had only half its original capacity because a wall was built across the interior to support the roof whose original design had proved unsafe. At this time, a colonnade was added to the entrance of the Odeum, and the six giant mythical figures located there have led archaeologists to call this structure the 'Stoa of the Giants'.

The monumental facade of the Odeum, with its three Giants and three Tritons, alternating, may well have been used as a lecture hall.

Eleven years later, Herodes Atticus built the Odeum (or theatre) which bears his name, and thus Athens could once more boast a hall worthy of the city's fame.

The restored Odeum of Agrippa was completely devastated in the raid of the Heruli, and many of its architectural members were used as building material for the late Roman wall around Athens. Early in the fifth century AD, the old porch of the Giants was reconstructed, and on the other side of a spacious courtyard a large and technically advanced building was erected. Until recently, archaeologists believed this to have been one of the last gymnasia of pagan Athens, but recent research has shown it to have been an administrative centre reminiscent of a miniature palace. It has been speculated that it was owned by Gedesius, brother of Athenais-Eudocia, the Athenian Empress of Byzantium.

Once more, we can see here the way in which the stones of the great days in Athenian history convey messages from other periods in the city's past.

V.10 South stoas

These stoas were not such imposing buildings as the temples of the Agora, but they were vital for the everyday needs of the Athenians and they marked off the boundaries of the Agora. The oldest is that known as South Stoa I, dating from the Classical period, which designated the southern extremity of the Agora.

It consisted of 17 square rooms with a double colonnade in front. The doors of the rooms opened outwards, thus maximising the amount of space within: this was also the usual arrangement in ancient dining-rooms, to permit the placing inside of as large as possible a number of couches. The ancient Greeks ate reclining on couches, which allowed them to eat, drink and talk at their ease. It has thus been surmised that these rooms may have been public dining-rooms -perhaps those which Socrates describes as being "in the Agora" and of which he was fond of talking. In the Hellenistic period, a simpler structure called South Stoa II was constructed on top and in front of the Classical building. It may have housed state offices. When Sulla looted Athens, this Stoa was destroyed, and manufacturing premises of the Roman period soon covered the site.

The Middle Stoa in the ancient Agora, a monumental structure which stood in front of the two Stoas mentioned above, also dates from the Hellenistic period. Between the South and Middle Stoas, on the east side, was a building facing on to the Panathenaic Way. Excavations have shown that there was a line of tables here, and it is believed that this was the street of the money-lenders. To the west of the Middle Stoa and to the south of the Tholos, ruins dating from the Classical period have come to light and may be assumed to have been public offices for administrative purposes.

Somewhere among these buildings, we know from literary sources, were the *Hipparcheum* (the office of the Commanding Officer of the cavalry), the *Poleterium* (the office of those who sold items and conducted auctions on behalf of the state) and the *Logesteriai* (the state accounting office). Further to the north, finds of a more private nature have come to light, including nails similar to those used in the making of shoes and similar objects. Clearly, this was the location of a cobbler's shop in Classical times.

The Middle Stoa, too, seems to have had public offices. Even today, models of tiles made in marble can be seen at its north-west extremity. These were the standards of length and thickness with which all manufactured tiles had to comply, and we are struck by the degree of control which the ancient Athenians exercised over the market.

V.11 The Stoa of Peisanax or Poikile Stoa

On the north side of the Agora was the most impressive and best-known colonnade of antiquity, the Stoa of Peisanax or Poikile Stoa. Today, only the foundations of this famous building, recently discovered to the south of the Church of St Philip, can be seen.

The colonnade marked the northern edge of the Agora and took its name from its founder, Peisanax, son-in-law of Cimon, who built it in around 460 BC. Its purpose was to provide the Athenians with a pleasant place to stroll -for which reason, also, Cimon himself planted shady plane trees throughout the Agora.

The Stoa of Peisanax is better known, however, as the Poikile ('painted') Stoa since, as we know from the ancient sources, it was decorated with paintings by the finest artists of the Golden Age: Polygnotus, Micon and, perhaps, Panaenus brother of Phidias. According to one tradition, Polygnotus of Thasos did his share of the work free of charge out of gratitude to the Athenians for awarding him citizenship of the republic. Among the scenes in the Poikile Stoa, all reminiscent of the greatest achievements of the Athenians, were the Fall of Troy, the Battle of the Amazons, and the battles of Marathon and Oenoe.

The Poikile Stoa was the meeting-place of the philosophers. It is said that beneath its imposing portals Socrates was in the habit of receiving his pupils. But above all, the Poikile Stoa was the cradle of what came to be known, from it, as 'Stoic' philosophy, as taught by Zenon and his followers. Within the beautifully-painted walls of the Poikile Stoa 'stoicism', in its philosophical sense, took on the meanings of stamina, of spiritual serenity, of simplicity of life-style, of freedom from passion and of a preference for the natural life.

Behind the Poikile Stoa were the houses of the rich Athenians, and this district seems to have been among the most aristocratic of the ancient city.

V.12 The Courts

The Agora had a number of courts of justice in ancient times: the Courts of Hylaea. The remains of them have come to light at various points across the site, and one occupied the area on which the north wing of the Stoa of Attalus was later built. Six voting disks for use by the magistrates in handing down their verdict, still in their ballot box, and a water-clock were found at the same point.

The courts of the Agora tended to be known by the colour in which the lintel of their door was painted. For instance, there was the *phoinikioun* (red) court, or the *batrachioun* (green) court. The judges sat on wooden benches with shades to keep off the sun, and the presiding judge - one of the nine Archons -stood on a high rostrum. The atmosphere must have been rather similar to that of a modern courtroom, although the speeches were limited to six minutes in length and there was a water-clock to make sure this rule was strictly abided by. The water-clock was a clay pot full of water, with a hole in its bottom which allowed the water to trickle into another, lower pot. It took six minutes for the top pot to empty, and that was the permitted length of each speech. Justice was administered in an admirable manner, generally speaking, and the art of forensic rhetoric was highly developed in Athens. Such fine examples of the speeches delivered before the courts as have survived are still a source of inspiration to legal practitioners today.

V.13 The Eleusinium

Along the Panathenaic Way, on the south-east side of the Agora in the direction of the Acropolis, was the Eleusinium in the City.

This sanctuary was the Athenian 'branch' of the great precinct of Demeter and Persephone at Eleusis. It, the Parthenon and the Theseum were the most respected sanctuaries in Athens. Each year, on the day following that of the Eleusinian Mysteries, the Council of 500 met in the Eleusinium.

THE RESOLUTION AGAINST TYRANNY
An allegorical depiction of Democracy crowning the Deme (Museum of the Stoa of Attalus). "If any person shall rise in rebellion against the Deme, threatening tyranny, or shall contribute to any act of establishment of a tyranny or shall overthrow the Deme of Athens, then whosoever shall kill such a person attempting any of these acts shall be free of any accusation. The Clerk of the Council shall write this law upon two stone columns and shall place the first in the entrance to the Areopagus and the second in the place where the Ecclesia of the Deme meets. For the inscription and erection of these columns, the State Treasurer shall pay out twenty drachmas from the Treasury of the Deme, in accordance with the resolutions."

117

Pausanias reports seeing two temples in the Eleusinium: one was dedicated to the corn-goddesses Demeter and Kore, and the other to the mythical figure Triptolemus, who later became incorporated as a deity into the Eleusinian cycle. These deities, it was believed, had taught mankind how to plant the fields and harvest the crops, and their kingdom was the wide and fertile earth. The Temple of Demeter and Kore is believed to have been built in Roman times, using materials brought from a temple to the same deities at Thorikon, in eastern Attica.

The Eleusinium was the finishing line for demonstrations of horsemanship and for the contests between *anabates*. In their difficult and spectacular sport, the athletes raced against one another on chariots which they had to board and dismount from in motion. Archaeological excavations have brought to light here inscriptions and figures related to the Eleusinian deities, together with the special vases -called *kernoi*- which were used for offerings made during the Eleusinian rituals. They have also uncovered inscriptions relating to the confiscation of the property of Alcibiades and his companions over the affair with the Herms: they were found guilty of having defiled, when drunk, some of the Herms celebrating Cimon's victories over the Persians and having mocked the Eleusinian Mysteries.

In late September, shortly before the festival of the Great Eleusinia, the Eleusinium was the scene of the *agyrmos* ('collection') of the initiates. It was probably also the place from which the initiates set out the following day on their procession to Phaleron, where ritual cleansing took place. On the fifth day of the festival, they assembled at the Eleusinium once more, to walk up to the sacred gate of the Kerameikos. There, they regrouped before taking the Sacred Way and marching in procession to the Sanctuary at Eleusis. In the last days of October, the women of Athens shut themselves up in the Eleusinium to perform the first rites of the *Thesmophoria*, the feast dedicated to Demeter Thesmophoros, 'the law-giver'.

V.14 The Mint

Beneath and behind the south side of the Byzantine church which adds a note of subsequent elegance to the ancient Agora are some remains of a large building dating from the Classical period. Inside it, we have found coins and other items which suggest that the structure should be identified as the Mint of ancient Athens.

The first coins were minted in Ionia and Lydia, in Asia Minor. They were made from a natural alloy of gold and silver called electrum found in the sandy bed of the river Pactolus in Lydia. The coins of antiquity were true works of art. Those of Attica, minted by the ancient Athenians in the Agora, stand out for their elegance and perfection of design. In the golden years of Athens, the drachma contained 4.5 grams of pure gold. The four-drachma and ten-drachma coins were in silver. For many centuries, the Attic drachma showed the head of Athena, patron goddess of the city, with the owl, her symbol, on the reverse.

V. 15 The Stoa of the Herms

In the north-west corner of the ancient Agora, next to the Stoa Poikile, was another imposing colonnade, the Stoa of the Herms. According to Pausanias, the Stoa of the Herms contained the sanctuaries of gods and a gymnasium.

The Stoa takes its name from the Herms which stood in its interior and in its precinct. These were marble columns on which were carved the head of the god Hermes and his genitals in a rendition which might be described as naturalistic. There were no other anatomical details, with the exception of the god's arms, depicted as small protruberances. Hermes was especially popular in Athens, and the ancient Greeks assigned him the role of protecting roads and gateways. That is why the columns bearing his name were set up in the Agora, at crossroads and by the doorways of houses.

Of the Classical Stoa of the Herms, the luxurious Mansion of Pulytion and the precinct of the craftsmen of Dionysus, only two inscriptions have survived. Without them, we would have no knowledge of the whereabouts of these buildings.

V.16 The Theseum

This was a large open-air sanctuary dedicated to Theseus, the national hero of Athens. This was the place that Cimon and the Athenians buried what were believed to be Theseus' bones, which they repatriated from Syros. The Theseum was a place of safety for fugitive citizens, and also for runaway slaves. Theseus was accorded honours equal to those of a god, with sacrifices, torchlight processions and athletic contests.

V.17 The 'Prison of Socrates'

Approximately one hundred metres beyond the south-west boundary of the Agora, among the ruins of houses and commercial premises, is a limestone public building which has been identified as the *Desmoterium* or prison of the Classical period. Very little building material is visible, most of it having been carried off. Among the finds on the site were 13 small pots, which may have been used to administer hemlock to those condemned to death. A small and badly damaged statuette of Socrates was also found. This evidence, taken in conjunction with the accounts given in the Dialogues of Plato and in Plutarch, lead us to the tentative conclusion that this was indeed the ancient prison and therefore the place where Socrates was incarcerated before being put to death.

V.18 The Enneakrounos

Among the other ruins in this part of the Agora are an ingenious water-clock constructed in the Classical period, the Enneakrounos -a fountain with nine spouts- and small-scale temples dating from the Roman period.

Under Byzantine rule (eleventh century), a charming chapel of the Holy Apostles

*THE CHURCH OF THE HOLY APOSTLES 'TOU SOLAKI', 11th century, on the Panathenaic Way
This is the only evidence of Byzantine Athens in the ancient Agora -a monument that time and
the archaeologists have respected.*

'tou Solaki' was built next to the Enneakrounos. After much alteration and expansion down the centuries, the chapel was recently restored to its original elegant form, as it was nine centuries ago. The cost of the restoration was borne by the

Samuel Kress Foundation of America. The chapel is of the cross-in-square type, with a dome supported by four columns. The floor-plan is rather like a rose. The masonry is of the highest quality, with cloisonné work (bands of brick in among the courses of stone) and ornamental motifs in niches.

V.19 The Library of Pantaenus

In the Roman period, a certain Titus Flavius Pantaenus built a library next to the Stoa of Attalus. An inscription found on the site tells us, "No books may be removed since thus we have sworn -open from one o'clock to six o'clock".

Those are the most important monuments of the Agora. History, however, had an evil fate in store for the Agora of Athens. First the Persians, then Sulla and lastly the Heruli wrecked and devastated its buildings, and over time the site acquired quite a different appearance. Whatever was left of its monuments lay buried beneath the soil, and one of the most romantic neighbourhoods of Athens came into being above them: this was the part of Plaka known as *Vlassarou* or *Vrysaki*. In Vlassarou there were six little churches to signal the triumph of Christianity over paganism. This was one of the prettiest corners of Plaka, until the archaeological excavations began and almost all the traces of the Byzantine era had to be sacrificed in order to retrieve the remains of the ancient world.

Old Athens has vanished, along with the churches, the houses and the people. Even earlier, the twists and turns of fortune had caused the disappearance of the ancient Athenians, too -the people who walked, talked and listened, bought and sold, voted and were elected, watched and judged in this place. Yet the 'thirty-two columns' -the temple of Hephaestus- are still firmly in place,and the Stoa of Attalus has been restored. Of all the other monuments, there are only scattered stones to remind us of the history of thousands of years -the history of Athens.

VI. THE KERAMEIKOS

After the Acropolis and the ancient Agora, the Kerameikos is the third most important ancient site in Athens. It functioned as the city's main cemetery from the early historic period until the late Roman era (that is, from 1100 BC to 150 AD), an uninterrupted span of more than a millenium in which deceased Athenians were buried on the site. Its name comes either from the hero Keramos, son of Dionysus and Ariadne, or from the fact that there were numerous pottery (ceramic) workshops in the area.

VI.1 The Cemetery of Kerameikos

The laws of Solon imposed on the Athenians the obligation to look after their aged parents and make arrangements for their burial. Any citizen who neglected this duty was made to pay a fine and lost his civil rights -which was tantamount to losing his personal honour. Much ritual was involved in care for the dead. The corpse would be washed, dressed in clean clothes -usually white- and laid on a bed or table with its feet towards the door and its head resting on a pillow with a flower pattern. The wake was kept by the women members of the close family, male relatives and friends. Dirge-singers, flowers, special funerary vases and pots of scent completed the picture of the 'laying-out' ceremony, one which was very often depicted on the funerary pottery of antiquity and which is still to be seen, almost unchanged, in many parts of Greece today.

A coin was often placed in the corpse's mouth. This was the obol which, it was believed, the dead soul would need to pay the ferryman who took it across the river separating the world of the living from that of the dead. Sometimes a honey-soaked sweetmeat was put close to the body: it would be needed to get on the good side of Cerberus, the dog who guarded the entrance to Hades. The funeral itself took place late at night, before the first ray of sun appeared and was polluted by the dead person, who was regarded as unclean. Purification ceremonies were held, and the family members washed in water brought from another house before sitting down together to the funeral banquet. On the following day, the house was purified with sea-water. On the third day, the ninth, and the thirtieth, and then a year after the death, offerings and sacrifices were made in memory of the dead person and a symposium (drinking-party) would be held. The last day of the *Anthesteria* festival, in late February, was called *Chytroi* and was the year's major day of commemoration of the dead - rather like the Christian All Souls Day. A gruel of seeds was made in clay pots (*chytres*) and had to be eaten before nightfall. All the Athenians gathered at the cemeteries to pay tribute to their dead, and they sacrificed to Hermes Psychopompus, the deity who guided the dead souls into Hades. At the end of the day, to avert bad luck, people said, "To the door, Keres, the Anthesteria is over"; the Keres were the goddesses of death.

In the Geometric period, the general custom was for the dead to be cremated. Over the tomb in which the urn of ashes was interred, the Athenians erected a *sema* -the 'sign', a large vase to mark the site of the grave.

By the Archaic period, the tall, slim, funerary stelae ('pillars'), each showing the dear departed person in profile below a floral motif or a sphinx, had begun to form a stone forest in the Kerameikos cemetery. A special note of elegance was struck by the numerous statues, some seated and others upright. The stone figures of the sleepers were shown smiling: there is no trace of the sorrow of death anywhere in the cemetery. It was as if the Athenians of the Archaic period had conquered death. Only the inscriptions, with their familiar Archaic simplicity -naivety, almost- remind us of the tragic fate of mankind and the grief of those left behind:

When you died, Xenophanes, your father, Sophilus,
whom you left in deep mourning for your loss,
set this up in memory of you.

124

All the funerary monuments of the Archaic period are of the highest quality and were made by the finest sculptors in Athens. In that period, Athens was ruled first by an oligarchic regime and then by tyrants. Under such political systems, a small section of the Athenian people prospered: these were the rich aristocrats, merchants and craftsmen, who, naturally enough, commissioned the monuments for their family tombs from the best-known artists of the city. For that reason, all the Archaic funerary monuments were of superb artistic value. Unfortunately, however, very few of them have survived, since many of the stones were built into the walls after the Persian Wars.

In the late sixth century BC, the rule of the tyrants collapsed and democracy made its dynamic appearance on the scene. Cleisthenes, who was among the first to put democracy into practice, caused a law to be passed banning funerary monuments, because the cemetery of Kerameikos, with its costly memorials to the richer Athenians, had become a symbol of social inequality and an affront to the poorer classes. The cemetery suddenly went quiet, settling into artistic and aesthetic suspended animation. Now the silence of death seemed to hang still more heavily among the tombstones of Kerameikos.

During the golden years in which democracy flourished in the Athens of Pericles, a frenzy of building went on up on the Acropolis, and the 'great city' was at the height of its glory. The smiling face of Athens began to wear a frown only in the Kerameikos, where the shadow of death reigned. The Athenians, rich and poor, began to erect funerary monuments once more. On each stone, the figure of the dead Athenian was depicted in low relief, in an idealised portrayal in which the face was given a highly spiritual expression.

The monuments are flanked by lions, sirens and vases, all carved in marble. The large vases (lekythoi) which ornamented many Athenian tombs were imitations of the scent-containers that were among the usual grave offerings. On the white

THE KERAMEIKOS

(I. Travlos)

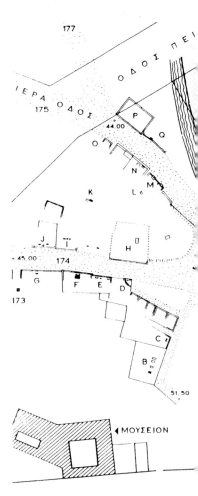

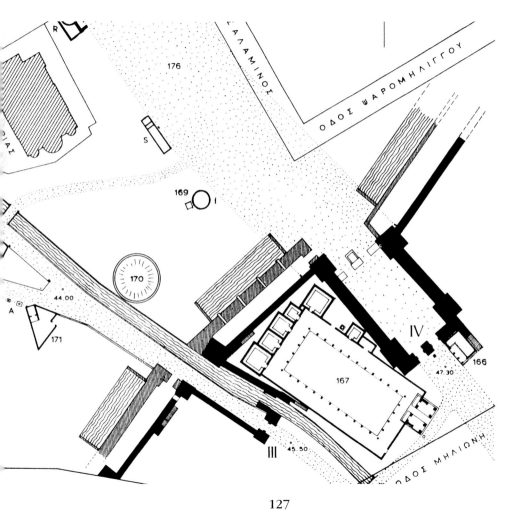

ground provided by the surface of each lekythos, the figures of Charon, lord of the underworld, and of Hermes Psychopompus can be distinguished along with the faces of the dead and their loved ones. The same themes were used in the white lekythoi of the great years placed on the tombs of the beloved dead. These lekythoi were the most sumptuous funerary vessels that money could buy, and on them the imagination and skill of the Attic craftsmen ran riot. In the deep gaze of the faces, we can discern dignified sorrow; these figures express the spiritualised idea of death held by the Athenians of the fifth century BC, as something which involved obedience to a natural law, but with the retention of all man's self-respect.

Apart from the usual offerings, many tombs contained what were called *dakrydochoi* -literally, 'tear-holders'. It was long believed, wrongly, that the Athenians actually did offer up their tears to their dead loved ones. In fact, these were microscopic lekythoi containing scent to accompany the dead Athenians on their way to "the harbour of Hades, where we all shall go".

In 317 or 307 BC, Demetrius Phalereas introduced another law prohibiting shows of wealth on tombs. Funerary stelae were forbidden once more, and only round short columns or small rectangular tables, in marble with inscriptions, were permitted. This ban marked the end of the flourishing Athenian school of funerary sculpture, and undoubtedly had an adverse effect on art.

VI.2 The walls of the Kerameikos

Inside the Kerameikos cemetery, we have an excellent view of the first few courses of the walls which defended the city at different periods during antiquity. The lowest of these courses, using small blocks of stone, date from the Wall of Themistocles. Soon after the Persian Wars, Themistocles became aware of the threat emanating from Sparta and, before leaving for that city in order to sign a peace treaty, gave orders that a wall should be built round Athens at the greatest speed.

The fortifications of Themistocles were later strengthened and supplemented with large, polygonal blocks placed on top of his walls. These were the walls of Conon, built in 394 BC. After defeating the Spartan fleet at Cnidus, Conon did much to make the city's defences stronger.

The topmost courses date from the repairs instigated by the great orators Demosthenes and Lycurgus after the battle of Chaeronea in 338 BC. Fearful of the new threat that had arisen in Macedon, Demosthenes urged the Athenians to build more walls, a gate and a moat to strengthen their city. This phase in the fortifications of Athens led to a notorious dispute between two of history's greatest public speakers, Demosthenes on behalf of the democrats and Aeschynes in support of the oligarchic party.

VI.3 The gates of the Kerameikos

The official gates of Athens were at the Kerameikos on the Panathenaic Way. They divided the area into Inner and Outer Kerameikos -where the tombs were- and were also called the Thriasian Gates, because outside them began the great road that led to Thria, the deme in the plain of Eleusis, also known as the Thriasian Plain.

The imposing entrance to Athens was later called the *Dipylon* -double- Gate, a name which occurs first in an inscription of the third century BC. Earlier, in the fifth century, the 'Gate of Themistocles' (as the first Dipylon was known) had the same surface area and ground plan as the subsequent structure. In the early Hellenistic period (307-4 BC), the gate was rebuilt, with stronger walls and a second double gate in front. On the outer side, the gate had two towers, of which the right-hand one protruded beyond the line of the wall a little further than the other. This made the gate easier to defend and had been a common practice since Mycenean times.

The Dipylon Gate was the largest city entrance in the ancient world, with a ground area of 1,800 square metres. This vast size was not a matter only of strategic or defensive considerations: religion was involved, too. The Kerameikos road began in front of the gate, and the kind of plaza there was used for funerary rituals (assemblies, sacrifices, athletic contests) in honour of the person to be buried in the nearby cemetery. In Roman times, too, the Dipylon was regarded as the main entrance to Athens.

On entering the gate, the new arrival in Athens would first see an altar dedicated to three deities: Zeus Herceius, Hermes Psychopompus and the hero Acamas. Zeus Herceius was the protector of the city walls, Hermes Psychopompus was, as we have seen, the keeper of the gate, leading the dead through into the dark palaces of Hades, and the hero Acamas, worshipped with these greater gods, was the founder of the Athenian 'tribe' which bore his name and to whom the Kerameikos area belonged.

Next to this altar, on the left side of the Dipylon, was a fountain dating from 307-4 BC, with comfortable benches on which those who had just arrived could quench their thirst and rest. It was usually for a symbolic rite of cleansing to be performed before the visitor set foot on the sacred earth of Pallas Athena.

To the west of the Dipylon Gate was another historic entrance to the city, the 'Sacred Gate'. It was given this name because every five years, in late September, it was the starting-point for the majestic procession of initiates as they set out for the sanctuary of Demeter at Eleusis. The road that took the initiates from the Sacred Gate to the sanctuary at Eleusis, where they would conduct the Mysteries, was called the Sacred Way. It followed approximately the same route as the modern street which bears its name (the *'Iera Odos'*), with a length of 22 kilometres and a width of five metres. The Sacred Way ran first through the Kerameikos cemetery and then passed the sanctuary of Apollo Daphnius and an open-air sanctuary of Aphrodite before running down to the sea at Lake Rheitoi, now known as Lake Koumoundourou. As they walked along this route, the initiates sacrificed at the sanctuaries and performed various rituals. They then purified themselves by washing in the water of Lake Rheitoi so that they would arrive untainted at the Great Sanctuary of Eleusis to honour the corn-goddess in the Mysteries.

Next to the Sacred Gate of the Kerameikos -a ruin today- archaeologists found a boundary stone with an inscription which proved that this had been the starting-point of the road to Eleusis. Also here are the remains of the vaulted channel over the Eridanus, the little river that ran through the Sacred Gate. One of the most celebrated rivers in ancient Attica, the Eridanus rose on Mt Hymettus and flowed into the Ilissus. Its name probably comes from the Homeric word *'erion'*, a grave, so the Eridanus is the river that runs through the graves, i.e. the cemetery. Over the centuries, the flow of water dwindled away until today there is barely a trickle, which lies stagnant among the ruins of the Sacred Gate. Tadpoles and frogs now play in the weedy waters of what was once a powerful stream.

VI.4 The Pompeium

Between the two Gates of the Kerameikos was an important public building: the Pompeium, where the preparations for all the Athenian festivals took place. The sacred utensils -the *pompeia*- were kept in the building, which was the starting-point for all processions and notably for the splendid Panathenaic Procession.

It seems that in very early times the preparations for the Panathenaic Procession and all the other festivals which involved the participation of all the Athenians took place on this site, though it was empty then. The earliest Pompeium was built in the late fifth century BC and was in the form of a gymnasium. Four elegant colonnades surrounded a large rectangular courtyard, and on the north and west sides there were at least six sumptuously decorated rooms. These were used for the official banquets held in honour of the delegations from other cities which came to take part in the festivals of Athens. The rooms had 66 couches for diners, and one of them yielded some of the earliest Greek mosaics, showing fighting animals (Room VI). Diogenes Laertius and Plutarch report that the Pompeium contained a bronze statue of Socrates created by Lysippus and wall-paintings of famous persons, including Isocrates and the comic dramatists. On the ruins of the east wall of the Pompeium, next to the door, we can still pick out various inscriptions left by youths, among which the name of the comic poet Menander is mentioned. At the entrance to the Pompeium was a majestic porch, and in front of it was a spacious square, where the famous Panathenaic Procession formed up every four years.

The Pompeium was destroyed by Sulla in 86 BC and rebuilt under Hadrian in the form of a three-aisled basilica. In 267 AD it fell victim to the looting and burning of the Heruli, and not long afterwards the last pagans in Athens erected some monumental structures within its ruins to serve the same purpose as the ancient Pompeium had done.

VI.5 The Kerameikos Road

The Dipylon Gate was the starting-point for the noble Kerameikos Road, also known as the Academy Road because it led to the Academy, "that most beautiful of suburbs". The road was 39 metres wide and 1.5 km long.

To the right and left of the street were the tombs of eminent Athenians. Pausanias tells us that he saw the tombs of Pericles and Aspasia, of the tyrannocides Harmodius and Aristogeiton, and of the famous generals Cleisthenes, Thrasybulus and Phormion. Unfortunately, no one knows what became of these tombs. At the

Right: 'HEGESO OF PROXENUS' a funerary stele of 400 BC (Archaeological Museum).

133

beginning of the street, by the Oros Kerameikon —the boundary stone which marked the spot— was the tomb of the Scythian physician Toxareus, who came to Athens in the time of Solon.

Near this, to the left of the Kerameikos Road, was the most magnificent of the memorials, called the Demosion Sema or Polyandreum. Here, the ashes of Athenians who had fallen in battle were interred at the public expense. This was the spot on which Pericles delivered his famous funeral oration -for preserving which we have to thank Thucydides- over the first dead of the Peloponnesian War.

In the vicinity of Kerameikos, out towards the Academy, was a small temple dedicated to Dionysus Eleuthereus. The god of wine was worshipped here by that epithet because his cult had come from Eleutherae on Mt Cithaeron. Once a year, shortly before the Great Dionysia, the devotees of Dionysus brought the cult statue of the god to this temple from the "most ancient sanctuary" on the south side of the Acropolis. In late March the cult statue was taken back in state, thus symbolising the advent of the cult of Dionysus (Bacchus) in the city of Athena.

Approximately in the same area was the Sanctuary of *Artemis Calliste and Ariste* ('the most beautiful and virtuous'). Part of the stone-built precinct of this venerable sanctuary has been identified at a distance of 150 metres from the Church of the Holy Trinity in Kerameikos and the area has been laid out as a little park. Many votive statuettes were found here, offerings from Athenian women to the goddess Artemis, whose many functions included serving as the protector of women in childbirth. Close to the sanctuary, at the intersection of the modern Nileos and Irakleidon Sts, was another small temple to the moon-goddess, erected by Themistocles. Here Artemis was honoured as Aristoboule ('perfect of will'), a property associated with the Artemis Ariste and Agrotera whom the Athenians worshipped as a vital aid to their military operations. Themistocles, who won the victory at Salamis, will have wished to show his gratitude to Artemis for being the

ATHENS IN ANTIQUITY, Leo von Klentze, 1862.
"A revitalised spiritual image of the original" (N. Lieb).

'perfect' adviser to the Greek leadership during the Persian Wars.

VII. THE ACADEMY AND THE GYMNASIA

At a distance of 1,500 metres from the Dipylon Gate, the Kerameikos Road entered the Academy, one of Athens' choicest suburbs.

The position of the Academy -where the city's oldest gymnasium was also located- has been identified with accuracy in the district now known as Akademia Platonos ('Plato's Academy'). The etymology of the name 'academy' can be traced back to the word 'Ekademos', which meant 'district belonging to Athens'. In very early times, the Athenian story-tellers invented an eponymous hero called Academus, who was worshipped in "the wooded suburb of the Academy".

All along the road from the Kerameikos to the Academy were the public tombs of eminent Athenians. At the point where the road ended and the gateway to the Academy stood, was a square in which the Athenians gathered once a year, for the Funerary Games organised by the Polemarch in honour of all the city's dead warriors. Sacrifices were offered to those who had fallen in war, and also to the tyrannicides Harmodius and Aristogeiton who killed the tyrant Hipparchus and were revered as the founders and benefactors of Athenian democracy. Their bones were buried near the Academy, and in the same place the city had erected a Memorial to the Heroes which was deliberately erected in the gymnasium so that young people might see it and learn from the example of the tyrannicides.

Pausanias tells us that there was an altar dedicated to the god Eros in front of the entrance to the Academy. The Athenians worshipped Eros and at a very early date deified and personified the concept of noble relationships free of all moral taint. That is why they honoured him, with Athena and Zeus, in the suburb of the Academy. The gymnasium of the Academy was one of the most important educational institutions of the ancient world, a place which has had a decisive effect on the subsequent course of Western thought -even down to our own times. The Academy reached the height of its fame when Plato was teaching in the gymnasium. He was said to have been the founder of the 'Museum' -that is, the sanctuary of the Muses in the Academy, where his pupil Speusippus later dedicated statues to the divine Graces.

In the flower-strewn precinct of the Academy were twelve sacred olive trees, the oil from which was sanctified and used to fill the Panathenaic amphorae presented as prizes to the winners of the Panathenaic contests.

As well as the precinct of Athena with the cults we have noted above, the Academy was also the site of two important altars. The first was dedicated to the local hero Academus and the other to the fire-gods Prometheus and Hephaestus. The latter was the starting-point for the torch-races: these were contests in which the runners held lighted torches. The winner was the athlete who finished first, of course -but only if he had kept his torch lit.

The Academy Gymnasium, like all similar sites throughout the Hellenistic world after the fourth century BC, was laid out so as to impress. In all the course of their brilliant history, the Gymnasia retained their original character of places where young athletes trained and competed. At the same time, though, their use as places of learning gradually expanded.

The Gymnasium became the training-ground for athletes in the track and field events, while a separate section called the Palaestra was reserved for wrestlers, boxers and athletes in the pankration. In both locations, physical exercise combined admirably with instruction in the arts and sciences, music and the dance. Each field of study complemented the other, and all together contributed to the physical, intellectual and spiritual cultivation of the Athenians. As teaching in the Gymnasium became more widely practised, classrooms and libraries were added to the training-grounds, and the concept of the 'gymnasium' broadened. Etymologically, the word originally meant 'the place where men train naked', but gradually it also came to mean a place of education.

The same gods were usually worshipped in all gymnasia: Hermes and Heracles. Heracles, with his reputation for physical vigour, was the divine patron of bodily exercise, while Hermes was the protector of intellectual education. Both figures together contributed to achieving the sublime objective: 'a healthy mind in a healthy body'.

Athens, with its superb gymnasia - the Academy, the Lyceum (in the grounds of the Rizareion on modern Vasilissis Sofias Ave.), the Cynosarges (at St Panteleimon on Kallirois Ave) and the later Diogenium (in Kyrristou St in Plaka) -was justly recognised as the 'educator of all Greece' and of the entire ancient world.

VIII. THE TEMPLE OF OLYMPIAN ZEUS AND THE ILISSUS

The Athenians of antiquity regarded the sanctuaries of the Temple of Olympian Zeus as being among the city's oldest monuments. The cults of the site were exactly the same as those of the north slope of the Acropolis -and the Temple of Olympian Zeus itself is both the most magnificent and the best preserved of all the buildings.

VIII.1 The Temple of Olympian Zeus

The cult which predominated on the flattened hilltop even in the very early historic period was that of the father of the gods. In the early sixth century BC we know that there was a large temple to Olympian Zeus on the site -and this must have been one of the noblest buildings in the Athens of the late Geometric and Archaic periods.

In 517 BC, Pisistratus the younger (son of Hippias and grandson of the much more famous Pisistratus) conceived the ambition of building an even more impressive temple to the 'King of Olympus' on the site. Work began, and the crepidoma (base) of the temple had been completed when the tyranny was overthrown. The Athenians, intoxicated by their new-found freedom and wishing to have nothing more to do with the works of tyrants, stopped work on the massive temple. When the Wall of Themistocles came to be built, the unshaped building materials that had littered the site since the time of the Pisistratids were used to construct the

THE TEMPLE OF OLYMPIAN ZEUS.

east arm of the fortifications, which ran in front of the Temple of Olympian Zeus.

In 174 BC, King Antiochus IV Epiphanes of Syria, wishing to leave a major building project by which he would be remembered, thought of the Temple of Zeus and sent the architect Cossutius to start work. But nine years later Antiochus died, and once again the Temple of Olympian Zeus was left half-finished. As if this was not enough, when the terrible general Sulla sacked Athens in 86 BC he carried off a number of Corinthian columns and a great quantity of building material to Rome, where it was used in the Temple of Jupiter on the Capitol.

It was not until 125 AD that things seemed a little brighter for the temple, and within a mere five years the pro-Greek Roman Emperor Hadrian managed to finish it. The sacred building was dipteral -that is, it had a double row of columns on each of its long sides and three rows of eight columns at the east and west ends: a total of 104 columns. That made it the most magnificent temple ever erected in honour of the father of the gods, and one of the largest temples of the Roman Empire. Around 131-132 AD, Hadrian came to Athens to inaugurate the temple and dedicate the chryselephantine statue of Zeus in its interior. Thus Athens acquired yet another fine marble temple. All the Greek cities and colonies sent statues of Hadrian to be set up in the precinct of the temple -and the most beautiful statue of all was that presented by the Athenians, which showed Hadrian being worshipped at the same altar as Zeus.

In the Middle Ages, the site was known to the Athenians as 'the Columns', and it had a little Byzantine church called St John 'at the Columns' to symbolise the triumph of the Cross over the pagan idols. In Christian Athens, the tall, slim columns of the temple occasionally attracted stylites —hermits who lived at the top of such pillars. Apart from the Athenians themselves and the hermits, the Temple of Olympian Zeus was the haunt also of Turks and Africans— and there is a folk legend which tells of three evil spirits of Africans who had their lair in among the columns.

The majesty of the temple with its 104 columns seems to have been too much for destiny to bear, and as the years passed the number of columns dwindled. By the early years of the Turkish occupation, only 17 were left. In 1759, Tzistarakis, Turkish Voivode of Athens, demolished the seventeenth column in order to render it down into lime which he used to build the large mosque that can be seen today in the Monastiraki district. The Voivode of Chalcis, although he had repeatedly taken bribes from Tzistarakis to keep silent, eventually denounced him to the Sultan and Tzistarakis lost his position. On 1 October 1852, a terrible storm burst over Athens with such violence that it brought down the sixteenth column of the Temple of Olympian Zeus.

The incident went down in oral history: "the time the column fell down" was the expression the Athenians used to distinguish between events before an after it. The Athenians also believed that the collapse of a column was a dreadful omen for those who lived nearby, since it released epidemics and other disasters. They connected the demolition of the seventeenth column with the plague of 1792 and the collapse of the sixteenth with the cholera epidemic of 1853.

On 'Clean Monday', the first day in Lent, the milkmen of Athens used to hold their annual feast. All Athens would attend,with tambourines and violins, and the town crier would criss-cross the city, calling again and again, "All those in fancy dress, all the people of the town, come to the Columns!"

VIII.2 The Arch of Hadrian

As an indication of their gratitude to the Emperor who had done so much for their city, the Athenians erected the Arch of Hadrian, beneath which the Emperor passed when he came to inaugurate the magnificent Temple of Olympian Zeus.

The Arch, in a quasi-Corinthian style, marked the border between the old city of Athens and the new quarter founded by Hadrian, 'worshipped at the same altar as Zeus'. On the east frieze, above the arch itself, we can still read today the inscription, *This is the city of Hadrian and not of Theseus*, while on the other side of the gate, in the same position, the inscription reads, *This is Athens, the ancient city of Theseus.*

In the Middle Ages, the Arch of Hadrian was called 'the princess's arched door' - perhaps as a reference to the Byzantine Empress Athenais-Eudocia, since the fine basilica by the Ilissus which she was believed to have built was approached through the Arch. In 1778, the Turkish commander of the city, Haji-Ali Hasekis, built a wall around Athens, into which the Arch of Hadrian was incorporated as a second gate.

VIII.3 The Precinct of Gaea Olympia

On the south side of the Temple of Olympian Zeus was a precinct dedicated to Gaea Olympia, the mother of mortals and gods alike. With the epithet Olympia, taken from her 'worthy son', Zeus of Olympus, Gaea was worshipped in this area from a very early date.

In front of the precinct of Mother Earth was a chasm in the ground. The ancient Athenians believed that in the time of Deucalion the waters of the flood had disappeared down this hole. Just as in the story of Noah, so in Greek mythology Deucalion, son of Prometheus, and his wife Pyrrha were the sole survivors of a terrible flood. When the wrath of the gods receded, Deucalion came to rest high on Mt Parnassus. A message came to him from the gods, that if he wished to revive the human race he should "cast behind him the bones of the great mother". Deucalion was able to interpret this at once: the 'mother' was the earth, and her 'bones' were stones. So Deucalion and Pyrrha began to throw stones behind them, and men sprang from the stones of Deucalion and women from those of Pyrrha. In this way, the stones brought an entire people back to life - which is why the ancient Greeks connected their word *'laos'*, people, with the prehistoric word *'las'*, a stone. This people was called 'the Hellenes' after Hellen, the first-born son of Deucalion and Pyrrha. The Athenians believed that the chasm near the precinct of Gaea was the place that Deucalion had cast the stones, and so they offered up sacrifices (though not blood sacrifices) in his memory and cast wheat-flour kneaded with honey into the opening in the ground. In this way, they honoured the figure who had regenerated mankind and brought into the world Hellen, to whom the Greeks ('Hellenes') traced their origins.

IX. THE BANKS OF THE ILISSUS

IX.1 The sanctuaries of the Ilissus area

Beyond the Temple of Olympian Zeus, in the direction of Athanasiou Diakou St, is an area with quite a number of important shrines.

The Sanctuary of Pythian Apollo is one of the oldest, built by Pisistratus the younger, son of the tyrant Hippias. To the east of this was the Sanctuary of Apollo Delphinius. The presence of the sun-god Apollo was important in this area, and here the epithet under which he was worshipped reveals his role as the patron of long sea voyages. It is said that Theseus came to this sanctuary to pray before setting out on the long voyage to Minoan Crete at the head of the 14 Athenian boys and girls who were the city's tribute to the Minotaur.

Naturally enough, close to the precinct of Mother Earth was the temple of her children, Cronus and Rhea. These deities were worshipped in a small Doric temple dating from Roman times, which the Athenians called the Cronium. An altar and a bronze statue of Zeus were to be found within this attractive sanctuary to the first Olympians.

Pausanias tells us that within this sacred area stood the Pillar of the Amazon, set up in honour of the Amazon Antiope. According to the traditions, Theseus fell in love with this warrior-maiden, and Hippolytus was the fruit of their union. The Athenians believed that Antiope fell in battle, fighting at Theseus' side.

A little further along, near the bed of the Ilissus, was a large temple of the Roman period which the Athenians called the Panhellenium. Here there were cults both of gods and of mortals. Pride of place was given to Zeus, the god of all the Greeks ('Panhellenius'), and his formidable spouse Hera. In Roman times, the Emperor Hadrian was deified and worshipped in the same temple -and on an equal footing- with Zeus, while his wife Sabina was compared to Hera.

On this site today there are only some stones and overgrown foundations to

SHRINES OF THE ILISSUS AREA

150. Shrine of the Poseidon Heliconius
151. Artemis Agrotera
152. Metroön in Agrae
154. Relief of Pan
155. Callirhoe
156. Ilissus crossing
158. Olympieum
159. Cronus and Rhea
160. Apollo Delphinius
161. Law court at the Delphinium
162. Panhellenium
163. Arch of Hadrian
164. Houses
165. Roman Baths I
181. Law court at the Palladium
182. Shrine of Codrus
184. Dionysium in Limnai
185. Palaestra of Taureus
186. Lysicrates Monument
187. Sanctuary of Gaea Olympia
188. Amazon stele
189. Pythium
190. Aphrodite in the Gardens
191. Altar of the Ilissian Muses

192. Cynosarges
193-4. Gymnasium building
195. Shrine of Boreus
196. Shrine of Pan, Acheloos and the Nymphs
197. Temple of Tyche
198. Stadium
199. Tomb of Herodes Atticus
200. Ilissus bridge of Roman date
201. Roman building
202. Lyceum
203. Lyceum baths
204. Gymnasium building
205. Temple foundations
206. Garden of Theophrastus
207. Baths of Diochares
208. Grave of Nisos
209. Heracles Pancrates
214. Eridanus
215. Ilissus
XVIII-XII Gates of the Themistoclean Wall

(I. Travlos)

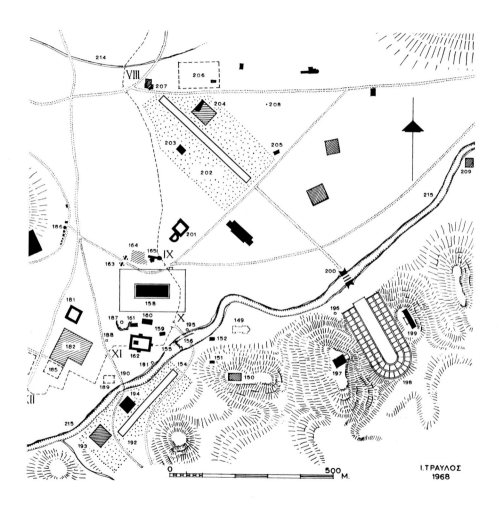

VIII

214

206

207

204

203

202

205

+208

209

215

186

201

164
165
IX

163

200

158

181

196

187
161
160

X
195

199

149

159

188

182

156

152

162

155

151

197

198

XI

191
154

185

150

190

189

194

XII

215

192

193

0   500 M.

Ι.ΤΡΑΥΛΟΣ
1968

145

remind us of these ancient sanctuaries. As we walk among the scattered trees, over the thin grass, it is hard to remember that this was once a verdant spot, with plane trees, osiers and flowers of all kinds, which the Athenians called *'the Gardens'*. They often came to stroll here, outside the walls, where the cool waters of the Ilissus and Callirhoe freshened the sun-baked Attic soil. Needless to say, such a sensuous landscape could not have been without its cult of Aphrodite, goddess of beauty. Here she had her main shrine, the Sanctuary of Aphrodite in the Gardens. The traditions say that the cult of Aphrodite was brought to Athens by King Aegeus. He also founded the Sanctuary of Aphrodite Urania, at a short distance from his residence close to the Gardens themselves.

The idyllic landscape of the Ilissus, with its dense vegetation and the "sweet clear waters" of the river, was a favourite place among the Athenians even in the earliest days of their history. It became a religious centre second only in importance to the Acropolis -and in such a place, it was only natural that there should be a cult of the Nymphs and Muses. Indeed, the Muses were often known as 'the Ilissidae', and were worshipped in a sanctuary they shared with the Nymphs.

Romantic Athenians often frequented the banks of the Ilissus, where they wandered in search of a place for contemplation and study. This is where Socrates met his pupil Phaedrus and where the famous dialogue between them, the *Phaedrus*, developed. In it, Plato tells us, Socrates invoked the gods of the sanctuaries by the Ilissus, and above all goat-footed Pan, and begged them to give him not material wealth but mental and spiritual riches, the true beauty which is inner beauty.

This idyllic landscape, close to the river and to the magnificent Temple of Olympian Zeus, was an ideal spot for the cult of Pan. In the rocks flanking his sanctuary, the ancient Athenians hewed out tiny recesses in which they placed simple offerings brought with great affection: lamps, statuettes, combs, pan-pipes and even tempting things to eat. They imagined Pan receiving inspiration and playing his pipes, the melodious flute that cast a spell over mortals -and that is how they depicted him on the rocks as the pride of his initiates.

The famous spring of ancient Athens called Callirhoe was once to be seen beneath the Temple of Olympian Zeus, near where the Church of St Photeine stands today. The name comes from two roots meaning 'good flow', and was quite naturally attached to the spring whose abundant water quenched the thirst of the Athenians of antiquity. Under Pisistratus, the Callirhoe area was landscaped in a monumental fashion and the spring acquired a fountain with nine spouts in the shape of lions' heads -the same pattern used for the rainwater run-offs of ancient buildings.

As time pased, the Archaic fountain became ruinous, and by late antiquity Callirhoe had lost its nine spouts. Yet even into the modern era, on St John's Day, the Athenian girls took the 'silent water' they needed for the ritual that would reveal the name of the man they were to marry from the spring, which had plentiful water. Pliny tells us that the water was "colder than that of the well in the precinct of Zeus". And according to the orator Isocrates, the water was so cold that the ancient Athenians used to add it to their wine to cool it. There was thus nothing unusual about the deification of the Callirhoe spring, nor was it strange that Phidias should have carved the figure of a female deity by that name on the west pediment of the Parthenon, among the other gods and demi-gods.

IX. 2 The Temple of Artemis Agrotera

In ancient times, the fine marble temple of Artemis Argotera was a distinctive feature of the Ilissus area. It stood on the southern fringes of Ardettus Hill, above the modern open-air swimming-pool. Notable for its elegance, this temple undoubtedly occupies a unique position in the history of Greek architecture. According to the myths, the goddess Artemis often went out hunting on the verdant hill above the Ilissus river when she first came from Delos, which is why her cult statue depicted the patron of hunting with her bow in hand. Here, Artemis was worshipped as *Agrotera* or *Agraea*, which means 'of hunting'. The whole area was called *Agra* or *Agrae*. The same area was also the location of a cult of Demeter and Kore. Every year, in March, the site was the scene of the 'Mysteries at Agrae' or 'Lesser Mysteries', the festival which paved the way for the Eleusinian Mysteries later in the year. Among the other rituals performed by the initiates was purification, for which they used the abundant waters of the river Ilissus.

The Temple of Artemis was strikingly reminiscent of the Temple of Athena Nike on the Sacred Rock of the Acropolis -which is not surprising, since it is said that, although earlier, it was the work of the same architect, Callicrates. It was a small and graceful amphiprostyle structure, with four Ionic columns on each side. Its white Pentelic marble must have glowed in the sunlight of Attica, and would have stood out against the green background of the hillside.

When Christianity established itself in the 'city of idols', it was inevitable that the little temple should change orientation, appearance and religion. Now it was dedicated to Our Lady, and in Turkish times the rather original-looking chapel was called Our Lady on the Stone. In 1778, it was demolished on the orders of the Voivode Hasekis, and its Byzantine building materials -together with whatever had remained of the ancient temple of Artemis, was used in the construction of the Turkish wall that bore the Voivode's name. However, it has survived in the drawings of Stuart and Revett.

Below the Temple of Artemis Agrotera was an altar to the wind god Boreas. According to a myth, the princess Oreithyia, daughter of King Erechtheus, was in the habit of picking wild flowers in the area. One day, the god Boreas -personification of the north wind- happened to see her, fell in love with her, and bore her off to Thrace, where he made her his wife and a goddess. The grief of the Athenians

OUR LADY ON THE ROCK, J. Stuart - N. Revett, 1762 (Benaki Museum).

at the loss of their princess was so great, runs the myth, that no wild flower ever grew at this point on the banks of the Ilissus again. Nonetheless, the people of Athens worshipped Boreas and set up an altar to him here, because during the Persian Wars a northerly gale from the slopes of Mt Pelion sank many of the ships of the barbarian fleet.

X. ARDETTUS

This is the name of the hill, 133 metres high, which holds the Panathenaic Stadium in its embrace. It takes its name from a mythological hero called *Ardettes* -who according to one tradition was such an inspired public speaker that he managed to put an end to the squabbling of the Athenians and helped them to live in peace.

At one time, the hill was called Helicon, and it may have been the site of a shrine of Poseidon Heliconius. In antiquity, Ardettus Hill was where the Heliasts swore their oath: they were the 6,000 judges of the 'people's tribunal' called the Helaea, and they vowed by the great gods of Olympus -Zeus, Poseidon and Demeter- that they would be just and impartial in administering justice. Above the marble-faced seating of the Stadium, on the right-hand side as we enter, was a temple dedicated to the goddess Tyche, with a chryselephantine statue of the deity. The temple was built by Herodes Atticus. It was in a corresponding position on the north side of Ardettus that the Athenians buried -with unprecendented pomp and circumstance- their great benefactor, Herodes, son of Atticus, of Marathon. They set up a funerary altar on which the phrase "to the hero of Marathon" can still be read.

X.1 The Panathenaic Stadium

In around 330 BC, the natural hollow in Ardettus belonged to an Athenian citizen called Deinias. When the need arose to find a site for a stadium, Deinias donated his land -without thought of personal gain- and the orator Lycurgus built the Panathenaic Stadium on it. Every four years, the Panathenaic athletic contests,in honour of the goddess Athena, were held in the stadium.

The stadium of the late Classical period was horse-shoe shaped, like its modern counterpart, but its seating was not faced with marble. In 134-137 AD, Herodes Atticus renovated the Panathenaic Stadium and installed the Pentelic marble, thus giving rise to the name *Callimarmaron*, 'the stadium of the beautiful marble'.

The length of the running-track (*dromos*) was 185 metres (600 Attic feet), and the competition field (*stibos*) as a whole was 204 metres long and 33.36 metres wide -the area designated by four boundary markers in the form of Herms. The seating was divided into two tiers, and had a capacity of 50,000 spectators. As time passed, the marble facing of the tiers of seats installed in Roman times fell off. The tunnel at the east end of the stadium was used as quarters for the beasts used for the circuses of Imperial times. In early modern times, the Athenians used the tunnel for the purposes of superstitious divination: it was called the arched hole or the stone with the hole, and it was said that "witches come here, springing out of the sea spray and the sandy beach at Phaleron when the night is stormy".

In the time of King Othon, the entire *stadium* -an area of land measuring 1.8 hectares- was owned by a man called Koniaris. The architect Ziller bought it from him for 2,000 drachmas, and in 1869 the first archaeological excavation of the site began. King George I then purchased it on behalf of the Greek State, for 10,000 drachmas, and a donation from the national benefactor Yeorgios Averoff allowed the process of restoring the marble to begin. The plans were by the architect Anastasios Metaxas, and the marble came from Mt Penteli as it had in antiquity. Once more, 50,000 spectators could sit in the theatre, and it was re-opened in 1896, in time for the first Olympic Games of modern times.

X.2 The riverbank theatres - Metz

Between 1870 and 1888, six theatres flourished along the banks of the river Ilissus, offering the Athenians cool breezes and something pleasant to watch on warm summer nights. There were also cafes with music: *café-chantants, café-aman* (where the music was more Oriental) and even *café-santouri*, where the principal instrument was the zither-like *santouri*. Some of these establishments were less respectable, being notorious for their private booths and glorying in the name *pandremenadika* -'places where the married men go'. In 1870, the Bavarian Karl Fuchs (the name is now Hellenised to 'Fix') opened a beerhouse in the area, calling it the Metz after the French town were a battle was fought in the Franco-Prussian War then taking place. Relations between France and Germany improved, but the name Metz stuck, and is now applied to the entire city district.

XI. PANKRATI

The area next to and above Metz is called Pankrati, a name derived from the epithet 'Pancrates' applied to Heracles and meaning 'he who controls all'. There was a sanctuary to Heracles in the vicinity, where he was also worshipped as *'Alexikakus'*, 'he who protects against evil'. In late antiquity, it was common for this hero, famous throughout the Greek world, to be worshipped as a kindly spirit who drove away evil, healed sickness and protected the dead beyond the grave, since it was he who had subdued *Cerberus*, 'the man-eating hound'.

The sanctuary of Heracles Pancrates flourished between the fourth century BC and the third century AD, and was located by the bed of the Ilissus river, on modern *Vassileos Konstantinou Avenue* between the Conservatoire and the National Research Centre.

XII. THE BASILICA OF LEONIDES (ILISSUS)

This is the earliest known Christian monument in Athens. It was also the first basilica to be constructed in Greece, marking the transition from the simple wooden-roofed churches of the Early Christian period to the majestic domed structures of the sixth century AD. It was built "in a place where many men had become martyrs" in memory of Leonides, Bishop of Athens, who was crucified at Troezen during the persecution of Decius (250 AD). The construction of the church is attributed to the Athenian Empress of Byzantium Athenais-Eudocia, perhaps between 423 and 450. It was the reason why Hadrian's Arch, leading towards the valley of the Ilissus, was renamed 'the Princess's Arched Gateway'. The basilica was richly decorated with works of the highest artistic quality, as we can see in the sections of its mosaic floor -the only traces of it to have survived- which are today among the treasures of the Byzantine Museum.

XIII. THE BATHS (BALANEUM) OF THE TEMPLE OF OLYMPIAN ZEUS

A total of 24 bath-houses dating from Roman times have been identified in Athens. The first baths were built early in antiquity and were associated with the gymnasia where the athletes trained. Most of the buildings were small, but richly decorated. The most notable of these buildings which can still be seen is that inside the site of the Temple of Olympian Zeus, near Hadrian's Arch.

XIV. THE NECROPOLIS OF MODERN ATHENS

"Our souls, like those of the ancient Greeks, approach the tomb not in despair, but in search of consolation and rest" (Nikos Velmos, 1927).

This was the rationale behind the laying out, early in the reign of King Othon, of the capital's first Cemetery, the first written reference to which dates from December 1837. In the funerary monuments that stand among "the guards of the dead" - the cypress trees, that is- we can clearly discern the concept of death as perceived, and still experienced, by the Athenians. The pagan Elysian Fields blend into the Christian Paradise, but present in everything is the shadowy figure whom the Greeks still call Hades, the underworld of Homer, the place where there is no consolation. The Homeric world of the dead, notes M. Nilsson, "is so deeply imprinted in the mind of the people that neither mythology nor Christianity succeeded in rooting it out".

The cemetery contains proof of the skill and enthusiasm of all the best Athenian sculptors of the nineteenth and twentieth centuries, from Christian Siegel (1808-1883), the Bavarian professor of sculpture in the 'Craft School' that was the forerunner of the National Technical University, to the nonpareil Yannoulis Halepas and Kostas Valsamis with his 'Occupation Mother'.

Among the great names are those of the Fytalis and Malakates brothers, Leonidas Drosis, Ioannis Vitalis, Yeorgios Bonanos, Ioannis Vitsaris-Tombros, Dimitris

Filippotis, the Dimitriadis clan, Lameras and, of the younger generation, Parma-kellis and Kalakalas. All these and other well-known or anonymous craftsmen in marble -all the artistic resources of nineteenth and twentieth century Athens- have produced work that stands out for its tenderness and melancholy.

Perhaps the most famous monument in the cemetery is Yannoulis Halepas' *Sleeping Girl*, on the tomb of young Sofia Afentaki (1878). The theme of the composition, a female figure recumbent on a couch or sarcophagus, goes back to Archaic Etruria and the Hellenistic period, while the execution, with its marvellous moulding of form, is reminiscent of Classical work. The figure is shown sunk in "eternal and dreamless repose". She has not been touched by the rigidity of death, the only allusion to which is the cross the girl is clasping to her breast. Halepas' Sleeping Girl became a favourite theme, and there are at least five repetitions of it, the most notable being that sculpted by Ioannis Vitsaris.

The Cemetery of Athens is beyond doubt among the finest galleries of sculpture to be found anywhere in Greece. Antoine Proust, in his *Winter in Athens* -written in 1857- rightly noted that "Greece reborn could be proud of an easy conquest if she had a regiment of soldiers less and a regiment of sculptors more"!

XV. THE HOROLOGION OF CYRRHESTES, OR THE TOWER OF THE WINDS

This octagonal marble tower was one of the most complex pieces of machinery that antiquity could boast. It was an amazing combination of a *'horologion'* (water clock), run off the waters of the *Clepsydra* spring, and a weather-vane, and it may even have functioned as a planetarium.

Constructed in the first century BC, the Horologion was the work of Andronicus of Cyrrhos in Macedonia. Early in the Christian era, the building was sanctified and converted into a baptistery. In the eighteenth century, it became the Tekke (place of worship) of the dervishes, and was adorned with green banners and all

SLEEPING GIRL, By Yannoulis Halepas. "Our souls, like those of the ancient Greeks, approach the tomb not in despair, but in search of consolation and rest" (Nikos Velmos).

the other trappings of Islam. Every Friday, the dervishes celebrated their rituals in the monument, culminating in their famous whirling dance.

Today, the figures of the eight principal winds chase each other in frozen but perpetual movement round the monument, which in its almost complete state stands out among the other buildings in the ruins of the Roman Forum.

XVI. THE MEDRESSE

The complement to the Tower of the Winds in its Turkish function was the Medresse, the Islamic theological school, built in 1721. In the nineteenth century, the building was used as a prison, especially for opponents of the political regime of the day. An aged plane tree, planted by the robber *Bibisis*, became the hated emblem of the prison and was celebrated in song: "On the plane tree of the Medresse no bird will perch, for its leaves are withered and there is poison at its roots". "Say goodbye to the plane tree for us", was what the prisoners would say to one of their number who was being released, and the phrase is still used -ironically- in Modern Greek.

XVII. THE ROMAN FORUM

The Roman Forum was a natural extension of the ancient Greek Agora. It was built, around 10 BC, with money donated first by Julius Caesar and then by Augustus. The founding of the Forum is recorded in the inscription that can still be read on the imposing gate that marks the west entrance, that of *Athena Archigetis*. The inscription notes that the gateway -with its portico of four Doric columns, in the centre of which was a statue of Lucius Caesar- was built by the Athenians with cash donated by Julius Caesar and Augustus.

The Forum is a rectangular structure measuring 112 metres by 98 which forms a huge atrium with an Ionic peristyle. The colonnades we see today date from the

*THE ROMAN FORUM, THE TOWER OF THE WINDS AND THE MEDRESSE, lithograph,
T. du Moncel, Paris, 1845 (Benaki Museum).*

second century AD, and those on the south and east sides are the best preserved.
To the south are the remains of a fountain and of a staircase which may have led
to an upper floor (where the *Agoranomeum*, the market police headquarters, may
have been). A second portico -Ionic this time- and a row of shops mark off the east
side, while to the north are the ruins of Public Latrines of Vespasian (first century
AD). The Forum flourished after the disastrous raid by the Heruli in 267 BC, when

all the activities that formerly took place in the Agora were moved here.

XVIII. THE WHEAT BAZAAR

In medieval times, the tiny church of the Saviour (known as 'Ayia Soteira') was built at the south end of the Gate of Athena Archegetis. The gate was now known as the Bazaar Gate because ever since Roman days it had been the scene of the annual bazaar where products such as wheat, olive oil and salt were sold. In the month of June each year came the time of the wheat bazaar, which eventually gave its name to the gate itself. On one of the pillars of the gate an inscription referring to these business transactions and to the imposition of price control can still be read. Later, the *narh* -the notice giving the official price of wheat as fixed by the administration- was hung here.

XIX. THE FETIHE MOSQUE

The 'Mosque of the Conqueror's Victory' was built in 1458, to honour Sultan Mohammed the Conqueror, when he came to visit Athens. It is believed that the site was originally occupied by an Early Christian church. Morosini celebrated his capture of Athens here in October 1687, and during the five months of Venetian rule the building became a Catholic church of St Denis. During the first period of Athenian liberation, in 1824, it operated briefly as a teacher-pupil school, and in King Othon's time was a military bakery. This mosque is one of the oldest buildings of the Turkish period in Athens, and is certainly the most attractive and best-preserved.

XX. THE LIBRARY OF HADRIAN - THE UPPER BAZAAR

The Library of Hadrian was built to the north of the Roman Forum in 132 AD, with a rectangular floor plan (122 x 82 metres). It had "one hundred and twenty

THE GATE OF ATHENA ARCHIGETIS, 'the Bazaar Gate' at the Roman Forum.

159

columns in Phrygian stone... and its ceiling was in gilt and alabaster", not to mention the statues and the paintings. On the ground floor was a *peristyle stoa* with special rooms for the safekeeping of papyruses and books, halls for lectures, debates and classes, and reading-rooms. The west facade had four Corinthian columns in its porch and further back, to the right and left, were seven more columns in the same order. The large atrium of the Library was cooled by a long, narrow pond with round ends which must have been an ideal spot for the readers and friends of the institution to refresh themselves. This striking building was partially destroyed by the Heruli in 267 BC and then renovated early in the fifth century AD. At about the same time, a beautiful church with a floor plan in the shape of a rose was built over the pond. Of sumptuous construction and with superb mosaics, the church is once more attributed to the Empress Athenais-Eudocia.

Some time in the eleventh or twelfth century, the porch of the Library was consecrated and the little Church of the *Holy Angels 'on the steps'* was built in what is today Areos St. The name of the church should strictly speaking be in the singular, since it is dedicated to St Michael. The church belonged to the wealthy Athenian family called Chalcocondyles. The Early Christian church over the pond was rebuilt at about the same time, being replaced by a Byzantine church of St Mary the Great. In 1720, the 'School of Greek and Common Lessons' opened here.

After the destructive raid of the Heruli, many of the activities of the ancient Agora moved into the interior of the Library. Under the Turks, it became the 'Upper Bazaar' and consisted of approximately one hundred commercial premises, thus making it the business centre of Athens. On the south-west side of the building, an earlier Turkish bath was later replaced by the Voivodlik, the residence and offices of the Turkish commander of the city. Facing this, in the direction of modern Mitropoleos St, was the Demogerontia or building of the Council of Elders - that is, the centre of Greek administration. In 1814, the Council of Elders erected a tower on the south side of the Church of St Mary the Great in order to house the "chiming clock" which Lord Elgin had donated to the city in 1811. After Liberation, the clock-tower became a prison, while the Voivodlik was converted first into a barracks and then another house of incarceration.

In the bazaar of Athens, one could find "intoxicating aromatic substances of all kinds", and there were *kamouchadika* which specialised in the most valuable kinds of cloth -though in among them were the *ambatzikida* where much cheaper materials were on sale. The steps in Pandrosou St, where the Upper Bazaar joined the Lower Bazaar, were the location of busy barber's shops. As a result of the shortage of physicians, the barbers were experienced tooth-pullers and appliers of leeches. On the facades of their shops were their advertisements: decayed teeth and boxes of leeches, testimony to their professional conscientiousness.

The bazaar of Athens hummed with busy traders and brought life to what had once been the Library of Hadrian until the dreadful night of 9 August 1884, when a disastrous fire reduced more than a hundred shops in the bazaar to smouldering ashes. The place where the heart of medieval, Turkish and early modern Athens used to beat was gone, never to return. Monastiraki, which reminds us of it today, has a unique privilege: it is the last reincarnation of the ancient Agora of Athens.

XXI. MONASTIRAKI

In the centre of Monastiraki St (at the end of Athinas St) is the little Church of Our Lady Queen of All (Pantanassa), a basilica built in the tenth century. According to a sigillium of the Ecumenical Patriarch dated 1678, the church formed part of a convent of nuns and was donated by a certain Nikolaos Bonefatzis to the Kaisariani Monastery on Mt Hymettus. It flourished as a dependency of the Kaisariani Monastery, owning property in the bazaar, and it came to be known as Mega Monastiri -the 'Great Monastery'. After Liberation, it went into decline and lost its fortune, whereupon it was degraded verbally, too, becoming the Monastiraki - 'Little Monastery'- of our own days.

XXII. THE TZISTARAKIS MOSQUE

"1759 he knocked down the column": that is one of the anonymous graffiti carved on the Temple of Olympian Zeus and the Temple of Hephaestus. The reference is to the Voivode Tzistarakis, who, as we have seen, demolished the seventeenth column of the Temple of Olympian Zeus to render it down for lime to use in building his mosque. Apart from being punished by the Sultan and losing his post, Tzistarakis was also blamed by the Athenians for having caused the epidemic of plague that swept the city not long afterwards: at that time, it was believed that the fall of a column allowed various epidemics and disasters to escape from the bowels of the earth to bring hardships to mankind.

XXIII. AVYSSINIAS SQUARE - THE YUSURUM

Since the early twentieth century, a weekly market for second-hand goods has functioned in Avyssinias Square. The square probably takes its name from a community of Ethiopians who once lived somewhere nearby.

Between the Turkish period and 1875, the district was called Manganaria, after the little Church of St Nicholas 'Manganarias' which stood there but has since vanished. The name Yusurum comes from the surname of a Jewish family of traders - the family of Noah and Elias Yusurum -who had a shop in the bazaar which can still be seen today. The whole area is where the street market of Athens is held, and it is particularly busy on Sunday mornings.

XXIV. THE HAMAM OF AMBIT AFENDI

The Turkish bath-house (hamam) of Athens is currently being restored in Kyrristou St, and is one of the rare examples in Greece of a building of its kind.

THE BAZAAR IN AREOS STREET, E. Dodwell, 1821 (Benaki Museum).

It dates from the fifteenth century -the first century of Turkish rule- and apart from its purpose of cleansing the body was also important in its social role, as a place for meetings and recreation, especially for the women of Athens.

XXV. THE KLEANTHES RESIDENCE - THE FIRST UNIVERSITY

In November 1831, two architect friends, Kleanthes and Schaubert, bought an old house dating from Turkish times in the Rizokastro district of Plaka from the Turkish lady Sante Hanum, repaired it, and moved in. The neighbours called the builing the little Acropolis because it was crammed with models of ancient monuments and architectural members from them. In 1835-6, Kleanthes leased the building to the state, which used it as the premises of the No. 1 Secondary School, founded by Capodistrias on Aegina in 1828 and now with George Gennadios as its headmaster. Early in 1837, a Royal Decree ordered the setting up of the first Greek University, and the Kleanthes residence was judged to be most suitable to house it. On 3/15 May 1837, the University was solemnly inaugurated. There were four faculties -law, medicine, theology and arts- and the 52 students were taught by 32 staff. In November 1841, the University moved into its new quarters on 'the Boulevard' (Panepistimiou/El. Venizelou St). In 1856, Kleanthes sold the building to a family from Crete. After this it changed hands often, began to deteriorate and even functioned as a taverna called 'the Old University'. As the intelligentsia had once crowded its classrooms in search of sustenance for the mind, now they sat in the taverna for more conventional food - accompanied by a generous consumption of wine. It was not until 1967 that the building came back into the hands of Athens University. Now, restored, it houses the University Museum.

XXVI. PLAKA

There are numerous theories as to the origin of the name 'Plaka'. The most likely seems to be that it is derived from the Albanian word 'pliakou', meaning 'old'. Historians say that at one time the area was uninhabited, its residents having been massacred during a pirate raid. When new settlers moved in, they included some Albanians who were guards in the service of the Turks. They called it the area 'pliakou Athina', which was gradually Hellenised to 'Plaka' and came to be applied to the whole of Old Athens.

The choregic *Monument of Lysicrates* (334 BC) might be described as the trademark of Plaka. In 1669, this monument came into the possession of the convent of French Capuchin friars and was converted into a chapel, later serving as a library. Even in its later history, the building never lost its beauty and was an ornament to the Capuchin house. It can boast of having lodged both Chateaubriand and Byron.

The Church of St Catherine is in the district called 'Kountito', a Romance-sounding name that comes from the French 'conduit d'eau' or the Italian 'acquedotto', both of them meaning aqueduct -and, sure enough, traces of an ancient watercourse have been found in the area. The church itself was built in the eleventh century and was dedicated to the Sts Theodore. In 1767 it became a dependency of the St Catherine Monastery on Mt Sinai, and adopted that foundation's saint. In 1882, the local residents organised a 'sit-in' in the church, demanding that the Archbishop appoint it as a parish church, and their campaign was successful.

XVII. ALIKOKO AND ST SAVIOUR

These names date us back again to the period of 'Frankish' rule in Athens and to two foreign families whose names became Hellenised as Alikokos and Kottakis. The first family gave its name to an entire neighbourhood, known subsequently as Alikoko, and the second to the main church in that neighbourhood, called St Saviour 'tou Kottaki'. The main street of Alikoko was once called the *'plateia rouga'* ('wide street'): now it is Kydathinaion St, from the ancient Deme which occupied the centre of Athens, the most beautiful part of the city: that round the Acropolis.

The Byzantine church of St Saviour was built in the late eleventh century, and may stand on the site of an Early Christian church of the sixth century. Kambouroglou, the writer on Athenian history and customs, believed that the church was dedicated to Our Lady as 'Saviour', and not to the Transfiguration of Our Lord, on which day it has its patronal Festival. The centuries-old popular name of the church as 'St Saviour' (in the feminine) is further evidence of this. After Liberati-

THE MONUMENT
OF LYSICRATES
(Plaka).

THE
KLEANTHES
RESIDENCE -
THE FIRST
UNIVERSITY.

on, St Saviour was the Russian church of Athens until the Russian community built its own place of worship. St Saviour underwent renovation in 1908, and that is the form in which we see it today.

In the courtyard of the church was the old fountain of the Alikoko district, about which many songs were written, but the structure there today dates back only to the beginning of the twentieth century. In Rouga Square -now 27 Kydathenaion St- is one of the oldest houses in Athens, described by Christoforos Nezer in 1833 as "the most beautiful of residences". It belonged to Ioannis Paparrigopoulos of Naxos, a member of the Society of Friends that had helped to bring about the liberation of Greece. Nearby, at 11 Kydathinaion St, is the mansion of Baroness Katakazi, a structure contemporary with the Paparrigopoulos house. For a time this was the Russian Embassy, before it too was bought by Paparrigopoulos. And at 9A Kydathinaion St, owned by the Seferiadis-Tsatsos family, lived a second-generation resident of Plaka, the Nobel Prize-winning poet George Seferis.

From Alikoko, we pass into the 'Chrysaliotissa Rouga', as Adrianou St was once called, in a corruption of the name of a chapel of Our Lady belonging to the Miseraliotis family (another Hellenised 'Frankish' name). The chapel stood at the foot of the street. At no. 96, the mansion of the Benizelos family, a typical example of an Athenian house built under Turkish rule, is still putting up the fight against time and neglect. Part of its garden is occupied by the Gymnasium of Diogenes of ancient times, founded to honour a Macedonian commander of the garrison of Athens who was regarded as having liberated the city when he abolished its guard. Heads of statues of the *cosmetes* (magistrates responsible for the education of youths) dating from the second and third centuries AD have been found here and are in the Archaeological Museum.

On the other side of the neighbourhood, in Thoukididou St (almost on the corner of Navarchou Nikodimou St), is a pre-War building which replaced an earlier structure of 1835. This is the Hill School, founded by American missionaries by that name who arrived in Athens as early as 1831. At the corner of Adrianou and Flessa Sts was the Mosque of the Column, on the site of which now stands a primary school designed in 1875 by the architect Panagis Kalkos. The older people of Plaka still call the building 'the school of Kambanis', after a gifted teacher who worked there for thirty years down to 1942. At 114 Adrianou Street is the No. 1 Girls' Secondary School of Athens. The site was owned by the American missionary William King. Nearby is another old Athenian school, the 'Academy of the Saviour' of Dialismas. It, too, served as premises for primary schools, and now it houses the Dora Stratou folk ballet. The presence of these schools has led to the street being called *Odhos Scholeiou*. At no. 5, on the other side of the street, is 'Church's Tower', a building which under the Turks was a *karakol* or police station. On Liberation, it was bought by the British historian George Finlay, who leased it to General Richard Church, one-time commander-in-chief of the Greek forces.

Up in Prytaneiou St, the eye is immediately caught by the Church of St Nicholas 'Rangavis'. This representative example of eleventh-century architecture was built by St Paul of Xeropotamou, grandson of the Byzantine Emperor Michael I Rangavis. The church stands on the foundations of a still earlier building, perhaps founded by Michael Rangavis himself in the ninth century, and there may well also have been an ancient temple on the site. The church retains its superb Byzantine masonry, the later interventions on which are very obvious.

On the same street, in the direction of the steps up to the Erechtheum, are the Dependency of the Church of the Holy Sepulchre in Jerusalem and the Exarchate. The pretty Chapel of the Holy Apostles was built in 1651 by a rich Athenian priest called Dimitrios Kolokynthis. In 1760, the building was conceded to the Church of the Holy Sepulchre and became a dependency of it.

Next to it is St John the Divine (eleventh century), a chapel of St Nicholas

'Rangavis'. In front of the churches is a flat space of ground where Morosini set up one of his cannon -belonging to the same battery that on the evening of 26 September 1687 wrought such devastation on the Parthenon. Above these holy buildings of Byzantine times, the nineteenth-century district called *Anafiotika* came into being. Here, in what had once been the 'African quarter' or the *'kara su'*, the 'black water' of the Ethiopian slaves imported by the Turks, immigrants from the Aegean island of Anafi —builders and marble-masons employed on the reconstruction of Athens— put up their illegal shanties. They erected two little churches which mark the boundary of their neighbourhood in its original form: St George on one side (NE), with its chapel of St Constantine, and St Symeon on the other (SW). The little white houses of the islanders, compared by one author to a flock of white lambs, struck a different note in neo-Classical Athens, bringing in a fresh breeze from the Aegean. Needless to say, Plaka is incapable of functioning in a city of 4,000,000 in the same way it did when the population of Athens was only nine thousand. Even so, for the romantics the district will always be 'the navel of the earth' —or at least the navel of Athens.

XXVIII. NEO-CLASSICAL ATHENS

In 1834, Athens was declared capital of the modern Greek state, the Bavarians settled in, and the message of the Classical Revival began to drift down to Greece. Greek Classicism was made unique by the fact that it combined an ancient tradition which had remained alive with imported architecture and an influence from vernacular practices. As a result, the neo-Classical buildings erected in Greece are light and restrained, with simplicity, balance, nobility and serenity. As the painter Yannis Tsarouchis said of the neo-Classical monuments: "They are flowers sent from the north. It is as if artificial flowers had been planted in pots and, under the sun of Attica, had —by some miracle— sprouted twigs and leaves."

SYNTAGMA SQUARE, drawing by Theophil Hansen, 1843 (collection of Apostolos Doxiadis).

from vernacular practices. As a result, the neo-Classical buildings erected in Greece are light and restrained, with simplicity, balance, nobility and serenity. As the painter Yannis Tsarouchis said of the neo-Classical monuments: "They are flowers sent from the north. It is as if artificial flowers had been planted in pots and, under the sun of Attica, had —by some miracle— sprouted twigs and leaves."

XXVIII.1 SYNTAGMA SQUARE

1. The Greek Parliament - the Old Palace

The Old Palace was built in 1836-42 to plans by the German architect Görtner. The foundation stone was laid in January 1836 by King Ludwig of Bavaria, who lent the Greek state 100,000 gold sovereigns for the project. The north wing burned down on 1 July 1884, and a second fire on Christmas Eve 1909 reduced the out at the same time, to plans by the architect Lazaridis and the sculptors Fokion Rok and Konstantinos Dimitriadis of Paris. The Parliament building was inaugurated on 25 March 1932.

2. The Grande Bretagne Hotel (Antonios Dimitriou residence)

This building was constructed in 1842 to plans by Theophil Hansen, and the Dimitriou family lived in it until 1856. From then until 1873 it was leased to the French Archaeological School and in the next year it was bought by Stathis Lampsas and Savvas Kentros for conversion into a hotel: the Grande Bretagne. After the death of Kentros, his share in the partnership was bought out by Lampsas, who was succeeded in the firm by his son-in-law Theodoros Petrakopoulos. The hotel was always thought of as the most luxurious in Athens. In 1960, it was extended to take the form we see today.

In 1850, the architect Panayis Kalkos built the Andreas Koromilas residence nearby, on the corner of Syntagma Square and Ermou St. Queen Amalia asked Koromilas not to build his house too high, so that she should not lose her view of the sea and he assented, for as long as Amalia was still in Athens. The café of Zavoritis, on the ground floor, was a favourite Athenian meeting-place.

In 1873, the businessman and intelletual Stefanos Skouloudis, from the island of Chios, and his friend and relative I. Vouros bought the entire block next to the Grande Bretagne -that is, the area enclosed by Panepistimiou, Vasileos Yeorgiou A', Stadiou and Voukourestiou Sts- for 400,000 drachmas. The plans for their building were commissioned from the French architect Y.E. Poitrineau. Vouros kept the corner part of the site, where the Meridien Hotel is today, and the Zacharatos café, on its ground floor, was the most important meeting-place for politicians and literary figures for eight whole decades, until the whole building was demolished in 1960. The Skouloudis mansion, which stood next door, survived until 1939, being demolished to make way for the King George Hotel (plans by D. Kalkanis).

THE GRANDE BRETAGNE HOTEL, formerly the Antonios Dimitriou residence, drawing by Theophil Hansen (collection of Apostolos Doxiadis).

3. The Pavlos Kalligas building (on the corner of Karayiorgi Servias St and Syntagma Square).

This building was constructed in 1910 to plans by Anastasios Metaxas. At various times in its history it functioned as the Ministries of Transport and Public Works. In October 1944, shortly after the liberation of Athens from the Germans, Prime Minister George Papandreou addressed a vast rally from its balcony. Today it is owned by Yeorgios Nikolaou.

4. The Old Parliament building - the Historical Museum

The mansion of the banker Alexandros Kontostavlos, from the island of Chios, was built in 1832 at what was then the north-east extremity of the city. In 1834, the government bought the building and added an octagonal structure. Until 1836, it was used as King Othon's palace. In 1843, when Greece acquired its first constitution, the building became the seat of popular power. In October 1854, the Old Parliament was completely burned down, and its reconstruction, to plans by Boulanger modified by P. Kalkos, was not completed until 1871. From this historical point of view, this is one of the most important buildings in Athens, housing Parliament until 1931. After that, it operated as the Ministry of Justice before becoming the National Historical Museum in 1961.

5. The Eftaxias - Vouros building, Museum of the City of Athens

(7 Paparrigopoulou St, Klafthmonos Square).

This mansion was constructed in 1833 by the German architects Lüder and Hoffer, as the residence of the Stamatios Dekozis-Vouris family. From 1836 to 1842, it and the Mastronikolas and Afthonidis (Beriketoglou) residences on either side of it were leased as the royal palace. The building was then restored to its original appearance by I. Travlos. In 1859, Dekozis-Vouros built a second mansion next door, at no. 5 Paparrigopoulou St, for his son. The plans were by the military architect G. Metaxas, and in 1916 the architect A. Chelmis made modifications to the external appearance of the building. Facing this, on Dragatsaniou St, was one of the finest neo-Classical buildings in Athens, the Amvrosios Rallis residence, which later served as the British Embassy. It was the work of the architect Stamatis Kleanthes. In the centre of the square was the Mint (later the Ministry of Finance), designed in 1835 by Christian Hansen. In 1939, when K. Kotzias was Minister and Commander of the Athens Area, these two buildings were demolished. Another superb residence, that of the Dimitrios Fotilas family, was built on the corner of Dragatsaniou and Stadiou Sts to plans by the architect Garnier, who had also designed the Paris Opera. The house was demolished in 1920.

6. The Anglican Church
This was built in 1838 to plans by Christian Hansen modified by Stamatis Kleanthes. It is a three-aisled basilica in the neo-Gothic style, with the apses truncated so as to give the building a cruciform floor plan. The church was consecrated in 1843, and is dedicated to St Paul.

7. Athens Cathedral
The foundations of Athens Cathedral were laid at Christmas 1842. The original design was by Theophil Hansen, and the project was continued by D. Zezos, François Boulanger and P. Kalkos. The Cathedral was consecrated in May 1862. The wall-paintings are by S. Yalinas and Alexander Maximilian Seitz, and the rest of the decoration is by K. Fanellis and Y. Fytalis.

8. The Residence of the Duchesse de Plaisance - Byzantine Museum
This group of buildings was constructed between 1840 and 1848. There is some confusion over the identity of its architect: it used to be attributed to Stamatis Kleanthes, but a recent study names Christian Hansen as responsible for the design. The residence was the winter quarters of Sophie de Marbois, and now it houses the Byzantine Museum.

XVIII.2 PANEPISTIMIOU - ELEFTHERIOU VENIZELOU AVENUE
This street was first called 'the Boulevard', and later came to be known -strange to think, today- as the Avenue of Acacias.

1. The 'Palace of Troy' (10 Panepistimiou St).
This is the finest example of the neo-Classical style as applied to secular buildings to be found anywhere in Europe. It was originally the residence of Heinrich Schlie-

THE 'PALACE OF TROY', Panepistimiou (Elefteriou Venizelou) Avenue.

THE NATIONAL HISTORICAL MUSEUM - OLD PARLIAMENT, Stadíou St.

mann, excavator of the sites of Troy, of Mycenae and of other Mycenaean cities.

The building was erected between 1879 and 1881 to plans by Ziller and the architectural concept was inspired by the Italian Renaissance. The ornamental paintings were by Yuri Subic, in a style reminiscent of the murals of Pompeii. Some of the finds from Schliemann's excavations are also shown. The building possesses a heating and ventilation system of a sophistication unparalleled in its time. In 1927, Sofia Schliemann sold the building to the Greek State, and until recently it was the seat of the modern Areopagus, the Greek Court of Cassation.

2. The Catholic Church of St Denis (Dionysius the Areopagite)
The foundations of the church were laid in 1853, and the design was by Leo von Klenze. The plans were later motified by Lysandros Kaftanzoglou, and the church was consecrated on 4 April 1865.

3. The Bank of Greece
This large structure was erected in 1936 to plans by Papadakis and Zoumboulidis. The strong rooms and the ventilation system were by the British firm of Faber.

4. The Eye Hospital
Since the world's first eye hospital was that of Vienna, founded in 1812, Athens was not far behind: the committee to set up the hospital was formed in August 1843, and the foundation stone was laid on 21 April 1847. The original plans were by Christian Hansen, after whose departure from Greece in 1850 the project was taken over by Kaftantzoglou. On the urging of King Othon, the building was re-designed in the neo-Byzantine style. The building was opened, as the Eye Hospital, on 14 June 1854. In 1869 an extra floor was added, to plans by G. Metaxas.

5. The Academy of Athens
This project was sponsored by Simon Sinas, who commissioned the plans from Theophil Hansen, and the foundation-stone was laid on 2 August 1859. Early in

PANEPISTIMIOU AVENUE, G. Mathiopoulos, 1904 (collection of the Athens Club).

1861, Hansen sent Ziller to Greece to supervise progress. In 1863 -after the expulsion of King Othon- Sinas discontinued his funding of the project as an indication of his displeasure, but after his death his widow Ifiyenia put up the money needed for the building to be completed. The superb ornamental sculptures are by L. Drosis, and the paintings inside are the work of Professor Gripenkerl of Vienna.

The solemn opening ceremony of the Academy took place on 16 December 1885, and Ifiyenia Sina offered to endow the foundation with the sum of 800,000 drachmas. However, Deliyannis -the prime minister of the day- declined her offer, out of a concern over what would happen to the foundation when the endowment ran out. A year later, Harilaos Trikoupis, who had succeeded Deliyannis as prime minister, approached Ifiyenia Sina to see whether the offer was still open, but in the meantime her businesses had gone bankrupt, and as a result the Academy remained closed until 1926.

6. The University
One of the oldest and finest buildings of neo-Classical Athens, one of the simplest and certainly one of the most magnificent, is that of the University. The foundation-stone was laid on 2 June 1839, and the building was designed by Christian Hansen. In 1843, all the activities of the University moved from the Kleanthes house in Plaka into the front wing of the building, the rear still being incomplete. In 1861, Sinas assigned the ornamental painting to the Bavarian Karl Rahl, but in 1888, after his death, the work was continued by Lebietski.

Until the overthrow of Othon in 1862, the foundation was entitled 'the Othonian University'. After that, it became 'the National University', and since 1912, in accordance with a clause in the will of its benefactor Dombolis -a friend of the first Governor of Greece who left his fortune to the University- has also been 'Capodistrian'. The facade is adorned with statues of the Patriarch Grigorios V by the sculptor Y. Fytalis, of Rigas Ferraios by I. Kossos, of Koraes by Y. Vroutos and of Capodistrias by Y. Bonanos. Closer to the street is a statue of Gladstone by G. Vitalis.

7. The National Library
In 1884, Harilaos Trikoupis commissioned from Theophil Hansen the plans for a National Library, although at the time there were no funds available to build it

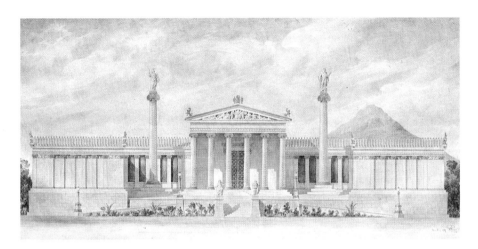
THE ACADEMY, drawing by the architect Theophil Hansen, 1859.

University'. After that, it became 'the National University', and since 1912, in accordance with a clause in the will of its benefactor Dombolis -a friend of the first Governor of Greece who left his fortune to the University- has also been 'Capodistrian'. The facade is adorned with statues of the Patriarch Grigorios V by the sculptor Y. Fytalis, of Rigas Ferraios by I. Kossos, of Koraes by Y. Vroutos and of Capodistrias by Y. Bonanos. Closer to the street is a statue of Gladstone by G. Vitalis.

7. The National Library
In 1884, Harilaos Trikoupis commissioned from Theophil Hansen the plans for a National Library, although at the time there were no funds available to build it with. In 1887, Panayis Vallianos contributed 2,500,000 drachmas and the Public Treasury came up with a further 500,000 drachmas, at which point work began.

Dimadis extended the building to cover the entire block, and in 1906 the help of Ziller was requested so that the baroque facade of the building could be improved.

9. The Serpieri Building - the Agricultural Bank
(corner of Panepistimiou and Edouardou Lo Sts).

The building was owned by the Italian Giovanni Battista Serpieri, who in 1864 took over the running of the silver-mines at Lavrio. It dates from 1874, and was designed by A. Theofilas, while the fine ornamental paintings are by the Italian Bilancioni. Since 1930 the Serpieri building has belonged to the Agricultural Bank.

XXIII.3 OMONIA SQUARE
The neo-Classical buildings which have survived in the vicinity of Omonia Square all date from the late nineteenth and early twentieth century, and most were the work of the architect Ziller.

XXIII.4 DIMARCHEIO - ETHNIKIS ANTISTASIS SQUARE

1. The National Bank
The Bank itself was founded in 1841 by Y. Stavrou, and in 1842 its premises moved to the "humble building" belonging to Kyriakos Domnadis. In 1852, the Feraldi building next door -which had been the Hotel d' Angleterre and was the best in Athens at the time- was bought, too. The facade which covers both structures was built in 1894 and may have been designed by Troump.

2. The Melas Building
This was a commission from Vassileios Melas which Ziller received in 1874. The building burned down in 1900 and after it had been repaired (by Zacharias Papadakis) it was taken over by the Greek Post Office. Since 1974, the National Bank has held a fifty-year lease on the Melas Building.

OMONIA SQUARE in the early twentieth century.

3. The Town Hall

In 1872, Mayor Panayis Kyriakos borrowed 130,000 drachmas from the National Bank and set about the construction of a new Town Hall to plans by Panayis Kalkos. The structure was completed in 1874, with additional financing from I. Kontoyannakis. The paintings inside are the work of Kontoglou and Gounaropoulos.

In the middle of the square in front of the Town Hall stood the famous Municipal Theatre, founded in 1857 to plans by Boulanger and not completed until 1888, with additional plans by Ziller and funding from Andreas Syngros. Konstantinos Kotzias, Minister and Commander of the Greater Athens Area, was responsible for its thoughtless demolition in May 1939.

XXIX. OTHER IMPORTANT NEO-CLASSICAL BUILDINGS

1. The Observatory

Work on the construction of the Observatory, made possible by a donation from Sinas and to plans by Theophil Hansen, began on 26 June 1842. The Observatory stands on top of the Hill of the Nymphs near the Pnyx. Hansen was so pleased with the result of his labours that he had the inscription *'Servare Intaminatum'* - 'to be preserved intact'- written high on the facade.

2. The Archaeological Museum

This was begun in 1866, to plans by Panayis Kalkos, and completed in 1880 under the supervision of Armodios Vlachos.

3. The National Technical University

This institution, standing on a site donated by Eleni Tositsa, was built in 1861 to plans by Kaftantzoglou. The project was financed by Nikolaos Stournaris, Michail Tositsas and Yeorgios Averoff, all of Metsovo in Epirus.

4. The Zappeio

In 1856, Evangelos Zappas, also of Epirus, made the donation with which this building -now a conference centre- was to be constructed. The original plan (by Boulanger) was for it to be sited beside the Stadium. In the end, the Zappeio was designed by Theophil Hansen (1879) in the form and on the site we see it today.

5. The Presidential Residence (Irodou tou Attikou St)

This building was designed in 1890 as the residence of Crown Prince Constantine, to plans by Ernst Ziller.

6. The Maximos Building

This was one of the last neo-Classical buildings to go up in Athens. It was built in 1924, to plans by Anastasios Chelmis, and completed by his widow, Irini Michalinou, who then married Dimitrios Maximos, from whom the building takes its name. It was bought by the Greek state in the autumn of 1951.

POSTSCRIPT

The treasures of Athens are inestimable in value. Each corner of the city is a legend, a piece of history. A book like this can do no more than provide a taste of the city. If the reader senses the allure of this magic city, if he has been inspired by some affection for it, then we have succeeded in what we set out to to. The "love of Athens, the legendary city of old" is a very powerful emotion. It has cast its spell on those who produced this book, and we hope it will have the same effect on our readers. If it does so, that will only be natural, for Athens can be summed up in one word: MAGIC!

THE MOST IMPORTANT MUSEUMS OF ATHENS

THE NATIONAL ARCHAEOLOGICAL MUSEUM (116)*
44 Patision St, tel. no. 8217 717
Opening hours: Monday 12-17, Tuesday-Friday 8-17, Saturday-Sunday 9-15.

THE ACROPOLIS MUSEUM (193)
Tel. no. 3214 172 Opening hours: weekdays 8-17, weekends 9-15.

THE ANCIENT AGORA MUSEUM (11)
Stoa of Attalus, tel. no. 3210 185
Opening hours: 9-15 (closed Monday).

KERAMEIKOS MUSEUM (195)
148 Ermou St, tel. no. 3463 552
Opening hours: 9-15 (closed Tuesday).

BYZANTINE MUSEUM (66)
22 Vasilissis Sofias Ave., tel. no. 7211 027
Opening hours: 9-15 (closed Monday).

BENAKI MUSEUM (136)
1 Koumbari St, tel. no. 3611 617
Opening hours: 8.30-14 (closed Tuesday).

MUSEUM OF CYCLADIC ART (185)
4 Neofytou Douka St, tel. nos. 7228 322-3
Opening hours: 10-16 (closed Tuesday and Sunday).

NATIONAL HISTORICAL MUSEUM (127)
13 Stadiou St, tel. no. 3213 766
Opening hours: 8.30-13.30 (closed Monday).

MUSEUM OF THE CITY OF ATHENS (124)
7 Paparrigopoulou St, tel. no. 3246 164
Opening hours: 9-13.30 (closed Tuesday, Thursday and Sunday).

NATIONAL GALLERY (173)
50 Vasileos Konstantinou Ave., tel. 723 5857
Opening hours: Monday-Wednesday 9-21, Thursday-Saturday 9-15, Sunday 9-14 (closed Tuesday).

MUNICIPAL GALLERY (110)
51 Pireos St, tel. no. 3231 841
Opening hours: 9-13 and 17-20.30 (closed Saturday and Sunday evenings).

ACROPOLIS RESEARCH CENTRE (78)
2 Makriyanni St, tel. no. 9239 381
Opening hours: 9-14.30.

WAR MUSEUM (194)
2 Rizari St, tel. no. 7290 543
Opening hours: 9-14 (closed Monday).

MUSEUM OF VERNACULAR ART (199)
17 Kydathinaion St, tel. no. 3213 018
Opening hours: 10-14 (closed Monday).

VENIZELOS MUSEUM (196)
Liberty Park, tel. no. 3213 018
Opening hours: 9-13 and 16-20 (Closed Sunday evening).

THEATRICAL MUSEUM (97)
50 Akadimias St, tel. no. 3629 430
Opening hours: 9-14.30 (closed Saturday and Sunday).

(*) The numbers refer to the map on page 190.

LEGEND TO THE MAP OF THE HISTORIC CENTRE OF ATHENS

ACROPOLIS
1.   PROPYLAEA
2.   PARTHENON
3.   ERECHTHEUM
4.   TEMPLE OF ATHENA NIKE
5.   THEATRE OF DIONYSUS
6.   SANCTUARY OF ASCLEPIUS AND HYGIEIA
7.   STOA OF EUMENES
8.   ODEUM OF HERODES ATTICUS

ANCIENT AGORA
9.   TEMPLE OF HEPHAESTUS - 'THESEUM'
10. THOLOS
11. STOA OF ATTALUS

ROMAN FORUM
12. GATE OF ATHENA ARCHEGETIS
13. HOROLOGION OF ANDRONICUS CYRRHESTES, 'TOWER OF THE WINDS', 'AEREDES'
14. HADRIAN'S LIBRARY

ILISSUS AREA
15. TEMPLE OF OLYMPIAN ZEUS
16. HADRIAN'S GATE
17. TEMPLE OF APOLLO DELPHINIUS
18. TEMPLE OF CRONUS AND RHEA
19. PANHELLENIUM
20. HADRIAN'S AQUEDUCT

21. PNYX - ECCLESIA (ASSEMBLY) OF THE DEME
22. PHILOPAPPUS MONUMENT

23.	LYSICRATES MONUMENT
24.	GYMNASIUM OF DIOGENES
25.	PANTHEON
26.	SOTIRA LYKODIMOU - RUSSIAN CHURCH
27.	SOTIRA TOU KOTTAKI
28.	ST CATHERINE
29.	ST NICHOLAS RANGAVAS
30.	ST JOHN THE DIVINE
31.	STS COSMAS & DAMIANOS
32.	TRANSFIGURATION
33.	ST ANNE
34.	HOLY APOSTLES 'TOU SOLAKI'
35.	PANAYIA CHRYSOKASTRIOTISSA
36.	ST SPYRIDON AND THE HOLY GIRDLE
37.	ABID EFENDI HAMAM
38.	MEDRESSE
39.	FETIHIE MOSQUE
40.	ARCHANGELS
41.	PROPHET ELISHA
42.	TSISDARAKIS MOSQUE
43.	PANTANASSA
44.	ST PHILIP
45.	HOLY ANGELS
46.	'CHRISTOS TOU KOPIDI'
47.	STS COSMAS & DAMIAN KOLOKYNTHI
48.	ST JOHN 'AT THE COLUMN'
49.	ST DEMETRIUS
50.	STS THEODORE
51.	KAPNIKAREA
52.	PANAYIA ROMVI - 'TOU ROUMBI'
53.	PANAYIA GORGOEPIKOOS - LITTLE CATHEDRAL - ST ELEUTHERIUS
54.	ST ANDREW

55.	'AYIA DYNAMIS'
56.	ARCHANGELS - CHURCH OF MONI PETRAKI
57.	BENIZELOS HOUSE
58.	FINLAY HOUSE - HOME OF GENERAL CHURCH
59.	ALL SAINTS
69.	PRESIDENTIAL RESIDENCE - 'CROWN PRINCE'S PALACE'
71.	OLD PALACE - PARLIAMENT
72.	KYRIAKOULIS MAVROMICHALIS HOUSE
74.	ZAPPEION
75.	PANATHENAIC STADIUM
79.	ANGLICAN CHURCH OF ST PAUL
80.	KLEANTHES HOUSE - OLD UNIVERSITY
84.	CATHEDRAL
89.	GRANDE BRETAGNE HOTEL
90.	ILIOU MELATHRON, SCHLIEMANN'S MANSION
91.	ROMAN CATHOLIC CHURCH OF ST DENIS
92.	EYE CLINIC
93.	SERPIERIS MANSION - AGRICULTURAL BANK
94.	ATHENS ACADEMY
95.	ATHENS UNIVERSITY
96.	VALLIANEIOS NATIONAL LIBRARY
97.	CULTURAL CENTRE OF THE MUNICIPALITY OF ATHENS
99.	ARSAKEION
110.	MUNICIPAL ART GALLERY
116.	NATIONAL ARCHAEOLOGICAL MUSEUM
118.	DOMNAZOS MANSION, HOTEL D' ANGLETERRE, NATIONAL BANK
120.	TOWN HALL
128.	OBSERVATORY
130.	BANK OF GREECE
135.	MAXIMOS MANSION